"A Practical Recognition of the Brotherhood of Man"

John G. Fee and the Camp Nelson Experience

Richard D. Sears

Berea College Press • Berea, Kentucky
• 1986 •

© 1986 by Richard D. Sears

All rights reserved, including the right of reproduction, in whole or in part, by any means, without permission from the publisher.

Manufactured in the United States of America

Berea College Press
CPO 2317
Berea, Kentucky 40404

First edition

Library of Congress Catalog Card Number: 86-71186

ISBN: 0-938211-01-3

Cover photo of John G. Fee courtesy of Berea College Archives

CONTENTS

FOREWORD by Thomas D. Clark i

PROLOGUE 1

I. THE PROBLEM OF CAMP NELSON
1. Fee and Camp Nelson 3
2. The Contrabands 4
3. The Eviction of Women and Children 10
4. Contrabands and Administrators 19
5. The Belle Mitchell Incident 31
6. The Legacy of Camp Nelson 41

II. THE SOLUTION OF BEREA
1. Berea's Black Settlers 44
2. Fee's Theories of Racial Relations 45
3. Fee's Policies: Interracial Education in a
   Community Context and "Interspersion" 47
4. The New School: 1866 49
5. Fee's Political Labors for Black Equality 50
6. First Term (January 2 - March 29, 1866):
   Integration of the School 52
7. Second Term (April 16 - June, 1866): Angus Burleigh,
   Soldier-Student from Camp Nelson 53
8. "Great blessings...to the African Race" 56
9. Third Term (September - November, 1866):
   Berea—A Success 60
10. 1870: The Fourth Annual Commencement of
    Berea College 64

III. THE PRACTICAL ACHIEVEMENT
1. Fairchild's Administration, 1869-89 65
2. The Ku Klux Klan 66
3. The Cooper Institute Meetings 68
4. The Issue of Intermarriage 71
5. Fee's Achievement 73

APPENDIX — Camp Nelson: Reverend Abisha Scofield
   and Reverend Gabriel Burdett 76

NOTES 79

Dedicated to the memory of John Gregg Fee

FOREWORD
Thomas D. Clark

Historians of the Civil War era in Kentucky have devoted too little attention to the complex issue of the end of slavery. The issue in Kentucky, a border state, was considerably different from that in the Southern states in rebellion against the central government. Kentucky was a sensitive middleground in the war, where any major tampering with slavery could have turned the tide against the Union. There seems no direct evidence that historians of the subject have known of or used the rich body of primary information contained in the papers of John G. Fee. This material pertains directly to the trauma of the dissolution of slavery as an institution in the border land. Tragically, freed men were thrust into a status of independence without having been prepared to savor the fruits of freedom. This collection of papers, part of the Berea College manuscript holdings, contains a gripping, intimate view of the knotty human difficulties facing Kentucky in 1862-1866.

In a general sense, slavery in Kentucky was neither a social nor an economic success. The Camp Nelson episode and the missionary work of John G. Fee and his colleagues was a concluding chapter in extended human history. Slaves brought over the mountains to Kentucky in the late eighteenth century from the older Eastern states proved good pioneers and made real contributions to the settlement of the Western country.

In many central Kentucky communities, slaves supplied the necessary labor to bring virgin lands under exploitation. Once the pioneer era had ended, however, labor demands were too low to make enslaved labor profitable. Too, there was a wide diversity of economic approaches to the Western country, with much farming activity only of the purely subsistence type. No single staple agricultural crop formed a central economic foundation for Kentucky. For almost a century, the institution of slavery was spread over a ragged geographical pattern, and institutionally it had a very mixed history.

After the Battle of Perryville in 1862, few Kentuckians could have thought slavery in their state would long survive. Looking back through the preceding century, few thoughtful persons could have escaped the anxieties slavery generated. It had been a subject of serious debate since the meetings of the conventions in Danville to effect separation from Virginia. Even in that era, the famous minister David Rice had published his stricture against the institution.

Since 1820, Kentucky experienced disturbing and emotional moments during the debates over the Missouri Compromise, the passage of the anti-importation law of 1833, the publication of a mounting volume of adversely critical literature in the form of domestic and foreign traveler accounts, Theodore Weld's *Slavery as It Is; or the Testimony of a Thousand Witnesses,* the publication of a mass of abolitionist pamphlets and, finally, Harriet Beecher Stowe's *Uncle Tom's Cabin.*

After 1820, Kentucky failed to develop either a staple agricultural crop or a system of industrial labor to employ profitably the increasing slave population. This fact subjected Kentucky to bitter social criticism, but, more important, it never seemed to be central in the heated discussions of slavery in public political assemblies.

Opening of the vast new cotton lands in the Old Southwest created an insatiable demand for slave labor and a ready market for slaves. This created a channel for a possible reduction of the increasing slave population in Kentucky. It involved, however, the social stigma of trafficking in human bodies in the interstate slave trade. This commerce was carried on between 1820 and 1860, arousing criticism and social guilt, but so far as reducing the Kentucky slave population, it made little more than an imaginary dent. The same thing was true of the so-called underground railroad operations across the Ohio. This latter drain was more sensational and provocative than effective in reducing the number of slaves in Kentucky. By the same token, various emancipation efforts bore only minimal results.

In 1860, Kentucky had a slave population of 225,483, and past census counts from 1820-1850 showed a rise from 80,561 to 210,981. Most slaves were concentrated in the Bluegrass counties. Although Kentucky did not fall technically within the terms of the Proclamation of Emancipation of 1863, it fell under those of the earlier Congressional act of July 17, 1862. This law decreed that slaves, the property of rebel owners, could be granted freedom by enlisting in Union labor battalions. Their wives and children might follow them out of bondage in the same manner, which meant they only had to accompany their husbands and fathers into the labor centers. The central point of assembly was Louisville.

Before the passage of the freedom law by Congress, the United States Army had already used slaves of rebel owners to build roads, drive wagons and perform other labors about military encampments, for which labors they won freedom. This practice created confusion and anxiety in the minds of both blacks and whites.

Union military headquarters ultimately became the "stars of freedom" in Kentucky. News spread quickly by word of mouth, and slaves and their families took to the road in search of freedom. Before the Civil War ended, the Army used increasing numbers of labor enlistees largely as an extra-legal means to emancipating the slaves. The procedure was instigated during the latter months of the war, because the Kentucky General Assembly refused to ratify the Thirteenth Amendment to the United States Constitution. This refusal seriously complicated federal-state relations and created needless political and social chaos in future years.

A dominant personality in the administration of military and civic affairs in Kentucky after 1864 was General John M. Palmer of Illinois. Actually Palmer was a native of Scott County, the son of pioneer emigrants from Virginia to Kentucky. General Palmer's father Louis was a rabid Jacksonian Democrat and a vigorous opponent of slavery. In 1831, he and his family joined the great migration from Kentucky to Illinois, where his son John fell under the same political influences as did Abraham Lincoln.

General Palmer had a fairly distinguished military record, and when he retired from active battlefield command, he was persuaded to assume command in Kentucky, where he served until 1866. No doubt Palmer's attitude toward slavery had been heavily influenced by his father. In Kentucky, he instituted his novel program of emancipation. He sought to emancipate slaves by the simple expedient of granting them "passes," presuming they would move north of the Ohio. He also supported the recruitment of labor battalions, an act which generated bitter resentment in Kentuckians. Negro recruitment seemed military in nature. And slave-owners looked upon the freeing of their slaves as uncompensated confiscation of chattel property.

After 1865, no thoughtful Kentuckian could have reasoned that slavery would endure. Remarkably, in spite of certain inevitability, no state or local plan was formulated to re-establish the freedman in Kentucky society. No one discussed how slavery might be ended after 1865 and cause the least disruption in Kentucky. The General Assembly contended that the federal government should compensate Kentucky slave-owners in the amount of $34,000,000 for loss of property. People feared that the freeing of so many unprepared blacks would result in outbreaks of violence, reduction of the labor force and a serious disruption of social and economic conditions. Few ideas in Kentucky history have been more exaggerated than the economic losses from freeing the slaves. The source of labor remained largely the same, and the great scourge of racial violence never occurred.

The concentration of liberated blacks in Camp Nelson and its vicinity in 1865-1866 heightened fears in the white population. Rightly or wrongly, ex-slaves were accused of petty thievery, pillaging public buildings, committing acts of violence and of general disorderly conduct. Stragglers along the roads leading to Camp Nelson and the Kentucky River were highly visible to the white populace, who feared they might wreak vengeance on former masters. The Kentucky General Assembly in June, 1865, urged removal of the Negro troops (freedmen) from the state, and later a delegation appealed directly to President Andrew Johnson to have the Negro "army" demobilized.

This was the political and military background in the closing months of the abolition of slavery in Kentucky. John G. Fee and his co-workers witnessed the hysterical reactions of central Kentuckians to the freeing of their slaves and to the concentration of black people in a federal military installation in the Bluegrass. In 1865, no federal agency other than the Army was prepared to deal with such a pressing social emergency. Neither was the Commonwealth of Kentucky prepared or willing to assume responsibilities for rehabilitating and resettling slaves in the land where they had existed for three generations. General Palmer's approach was a novel one, but it was met from the outset with local suspicion, scorn and resistance. The General was even accused of *selling* his passes.

The Fee manuscripts are eloquent in documenting the social chaos during the trauma of this social and economic transition. No one was more victimized by the turn of the national and state historical screw than the ex-slaves. Thousands of those unfortunates were cut loose from their anchorages of home and livelihood and set upon the land without claim to it and without firm notions of the meanings and responsibilities of freedom. That march to Camp Nelson in 1865-1866 was, in fact, a trail of tears for an innocent, victimized people who suffered from forces and circumstances over which they had no control and which they could not understand. No one in Kentucky in these months seems to have been more fully aware of this than John G. Fee. Fortunately, the military command in the Kentucky department was reasonably co-operative in support of his program in its earlier phases.

Fee and his co-workers exhibited enormous courage in assuming the task of helping slaves prepare themselves for their new lives. Beyond this, the task of dealing with the freedmen proved almost too great for the United States Government and powerful private humanitarian organizations. Perhaps John G. Fee took the only possible way in his emphasis upon religion and an educational program for people willfully kept in ignorance. The situation at Camp Nelson was complicated by two main facts: first, the personnel of the Army underwent frequent changes, and, second, the influx of ex-slave families all but overwhelmed the capacity of the camp.

This organized narrative, based on the Fee and Berea manuscripts, constitutes a remarkably clear insight into one of Kentucky's most troubling and dramatic moments. The documentary materials reveal a new dimension to the complex matter of emancipation of slavery in the South and to the absorption of freedmen into a regional economy and society. This material will stimulate a re-examination and rewriting of a vital chapter in Kentucky Civil War and Reconstruction history. Implications of this well-chosen and -edited text extend beyond the chronological moment of the narrative. The whole history of racial relations in Kentucky is placed in a fresh, imaginative perspective. The old hatreds, the public revulsions and the chaotic ending of slavery had ramifications well into the next century in politics, co-racial education and the desegregation of Kentucky institutions.

More locally, John G. Fee's labors at Camp Nelson and at Berea resulted in his return to Berea College, to renew direction of that institution in the post-slavery years. There lingered on in Kentucky for many years hatreds and prejudices generated by the labor act of Congress, the adoption of the Thirteenth Amendment, the actions of General John M. Palmer and the crusade at Camp Nelson.

The section of this study describing post-Civil War Berea College is as revealing as that on Camp Nelson's history. Here again, the material has a much broader application than to the history of a struggling missionary school in rural Kentucky. The contemporary insights into Berea's development also describe the reweaving of the fabric of the South in a new era of racial and social relationships. Issues raised in these years have haunted Kentucky and the nation for the last century.

In the final analysis, the success of John G. Fee and his fellow laborers demonstrated eloquently that humanitarian ideas have a powerful capacity to survive in the face of almost insuperable odds and to blossom. This study is a new contribution to the history of Berea College's formative experiences after the Civil War. The narrative reveals in documentary depth both the mind of Kentucky and the American missionary mind.

Professor Richard Sears has produced a significant text. He has done yeoman service in examining and interpreting primary sources. The tone of his narrative is clear and judicious. A book of this kind comes along only once or twice in a generation, and *"A Practical Recognition of the Brotherhood of Man"* has seminal promise of being read and cited many times over in future reassessments of Kentucky's past.

Lexington, Ky.
April, 1985

PROLOGUE

From fall, 1854, to December, 1859, John G. Fee lived and worked in Berea, a small town he had founded with the help of Cassius M. Clay in Madison County, Kentucky. As a missionary sponsored by the American Missionary Association, Fee had organized in Berea an antislavery, anti-sectarian, and fully integrated church, with slave members communing on an equal basis with their free fellow Christians. Fee's work attracted other abolitionists, particularly from Oberlin, Ohio, to the area, and eventually he attempted to found a colony and college in Berea: the school was to be open to all, but its special mission was to the poor, to black people (free and slave) and to women. Before the institution could open (late in 1859), irate Madison County slaveowners drove the Bereans, Fee and all his supporters, out of the state. In his exile, Fee resided in Ohio near the Kentucky border for six years, waiting to resume his mission to his native Kentucky. Union victories enabled Fee to reside in Berea again by 1865, but then a whole new field of ministry opened to him.

Since conversion to evangelical abolitionism in college, Fee had sought to help black people. He had always sympathized with slaves, and he wanted *more* for them than simply freedom from bondage: equal rights, education, economic power, fulfilling work, land and other property, religious freedom. When Kentucky slaves gathered at Camp Nelson in Jessamine County, Fee saw a matchless opportunity for service. For two years he divided his labors between Camp Nelson and Berea.

From 1866, the newly reopened school at Berea became his chief work, but for decades Berea was nourished by Camp Nelson. To understand Berea College and its place in the history of higher education in America, we must understand Fee's work among the contrabands at Camp Nelson.

Shacks, tents and barracks — Camp Nelson living quarters, 1864.
Courtesy of Berea College Archives/University of Kentucky Photographic Archives

I. THE PROBLEM OF CAMP NELSON

1. Fee and Camp Nelson

Beginning in March, 1864, Kentucky blacks were recruited into the Union Army. Within months, more than 1500 slave men had gathered at Camp Nelson in Jessamine County, and, before the year was over, about 5000 black soldiers had been trained there. "By the war's end, according to one estimate, between nine and ten thousand slaves — about two in every five Kentucky black soldiers — passed through Camp Nelson." The relationship of John G. Fee to the blacks of Camp Nelson, beginning in the summer, 1864, constitutes one of the significant formative aspects of early Berea and certainly the most neglected part of Berea College history.[1]

Camp Nelson is not connected to Berea simply because Fee worked in both places. From 1866 to 1904 Berea College, as a pioneering interracial institution, was the direct beneficiary of Fee's Camp Nelson work, both theoretically and practically. A central aspect of Berea's development is inexplicable without reference to Camp Nelson's brief, dramatic history.

Almost from the beginning, Fee was part of Camp Nelson. The opening of the main Kentucky military camp for blacks in a place easily accessible to him led Fee to assume that God was calling him to a ministry among the contrabands. In exile from Berea, where he had planned to open a college before the Civil War, Fee had saved himself for special work, and Camp Nelson seemed providential. From the time blacks began to enlist in the Union Army until Berea's reopening in 1866, Fee's primary work was at Camp Nelson.

In June, 1864, he began writing to the American Missionary Association, which had financed his former church-building work in central Kentucky, about new labors at the military camp. Five weeks in a row he wrote, receiving no answer to his proposals. In July, he decided to act on his own. He went to Camp Nelson, accompanied only by his 15-year-old son Burritt, without the assurance of American Missionary Association assistance, and offered his services.[2]

Captain T. E. Hall, camp quartermaster, greeted Fee's unexpected appearance with enthusiasm. "Soon as I came," Fee wrote, "he said you are just the man I wanted to see — I want three things — Religious instruction for this people, schools and clothing,...barracks for these people...." To the unresponsive American Missionary Association, Fee reported, "I agreed to meet the demands for all. I felt I must for reasons apparent to you at once. What will you say to me? Hall wants all the non-commissioned officers taught to read & write as soon as possbile." With the help only of Burritt, Fee undertook the tasks, setting up two tents to begin the school. "I must go forward," Fee said, "no [one] else here to meet this vast want. Berea at present is small compared with this. Both must go [on]."[3]

2. The Contrabands

Five thousand ex-slaves lived at Camp Nelson when Fee arrived, and more arrived daily. Fee began preaching to the black soldiers on his second night in camp. "This was to me," he wrote, "and to many of these men, a melting occasion." He saw then "'the beginning of the end' — the freedom of men, white and colored, freedom in such manner as would give prestige to the latter and sympathy from the former." For awhile, Fee preached every night; many of the blacks knew him already; "hundreds from Madison co. — most all," he wrote, "have heard of me as their *friend* [double underlining]. They *crowd* to hear me — a thousand at a time...."[4]

Captain Hall believed — and Fee agreed with him — that Camp Nelson would become the general rendezvous for ex-slaves for the entire state of Kentucky. Fee also thought it would become a future school for blacks.[5]

"I must act for this people," he stated. Fee's entire life's work as an abolitionist and reformer seemed to be reaching a climax.[6]

His own family was in need. Staples had become terribly expensive: flour $10 per barrel, only available fifteen miles from Berea. The Fees had to buy a cow, which would set them back at least $50. "I *need* money," Fee stated emphatically. It was a plea he was forced to reiterate to the point of humiliation for years to come.[7]

Slaves were enrolled as soldiers, uniformed and drilled as soon as possible in the camp. Fee enthusiastically described the men he saw at Camp Nelson: "...if there be a class of men in this nation which promises great good to this nation, in that class will be found these Kentucky colored soldiers." Some three or four hundred of the first colored regiment organized were from Madison County; they and many ex-slaves from surrounding counties knew Fee "as their friend," a fact he often noted with understandable satisfaction. He *was* their friend, and his open concern for their welfare — physical, mental and spiritually — never faltered through months and finally years of arduous, self-sacrificing labor.[8]

First, he was their teacher. Beginning with the non-commissioned officers, he taught them to read and write. "Most of them know their letters," Fee said, "quite a number could spell a little, and some few could read....The pupils are making astonishing progress, considering the small facilities they have had."⁹

In addition, he was their preacher. "I am here a voluntary missionary in the camps," Fee wrote "My hearers are not those of one regiment but several — if life and health shall be continued I shall reach many thousands." He had written approval from the principal camp commandants for his work. "I have no embarrassment in this most promising work of my life," Fee maintained, "but the want of colaborers — books. For the latter I think I shall not wait long." Although he had begun in two tents, he would soon have good schoolrooms in permanent government buildings and a fixed place for preaching.¹⁰

"I rode out through the camp (six miles in circumference)," Fee reported. On his ride he observed no drunkenness and no card-playing among the black troops. As he proceeded, the men "spoke freely and contrasted the present with the past....At nights," Fee said, "the camps of these colored men are scenes of continual prayer and praise with frequent preaching." As their preacher, Fee felt privileged to work with people whose piety was so fervent and so responsive to his own. Never in his ministry to slaves does Fee reveal a motivation of mere duty: he was attracted by the black people he worked with — in fact, he seems to have been drawn to them very naturally, with an unlabored sincerity and kindness that endeared him permanently to black people who knew him. Indeed, from the time of Camp Nelson on, Fee had a loyal following of blacks who never deserted him, whose love endured beyond his death. This relationship resulted not so much from his theory of racial equality as from his consistent practical application of it.¹¹

Besides functioning as teacher and preacher at Camp Nelson, Fee also served as a protector and defender for those whose lack of experience, and of legal and social status, made them virtually helpless in a difficult world. Camp Nelson housed not just soldiers but women and children as well. "Slave wives and mothers, often accompanied by children, in unknown numbers either visited Camp Nelson or fled their owners to the military station." Through Cincinnati charitable organizations, Fee worked to get clothing for the women and children. Commander Speed Smith Fry, faced with what he labeled the "Nigger Woman Question," had some of them whipped and expelled, but hardly a day passed in the summer of 1864 "without bringing...wives, children and relatives into the camp, either on visits or in pursuit of new homes."¹²

Fee sympathized with the slave families, many of whom had been beaten and driven off by masters enraged by the enlistment of their former slave men. Women and children came to the camp, Fee thought, because of "affection to the husband or father." Many black men on their way to enlist brought their families with them, to rescue the women and children from irate masters. From the beginning, recruiters had "somewhat inadvertently created camps and 'villages' of black dependents along with regiments of black soldiers."[13]

But time and again, Fry drove the unwanted refugees out of camp; some white officers expressed fears that black women would spread venereal disease among the black soldiers. (General Speed Smith Fry by order no. 19, August 25, 1864, expelled all Kentucky Negro women, but not those from other states. "All officers having negro women in their employment will deliver them up to the patrol to be brought to...headquarters.") The women were ordered to return to their masters, but those evicted soon returned, to be driven out again. "They would return," Fee wrote, "no place of shelter, and often their husbands gone they were much exposed to temptation."[14]

In August, Fee received slates, copy books and other supplies from Louisville, along with donated clothing. He wrote to the American Missionary Association, asking for undergarments for the women, although at that point most had been evicted.

Fee sought a teacher for Berea (he had tentatively secured the services of Joel Morgan Partridge, a former Oberlin student), and a preacher to pastor churches in Bracken and Lewis Counties, where Fee's missionary labors in Kentucky had begun. In addition he was preaching, teaching, superintending, corresponding and writing articles for Camp Nelson. The work, although extremely heavy, was gratifying, because of improvements Fee could point to — by August, for example, he had a new schoolroom, 80 by 30 feet. And he had begun to conceive new plans. On August 1, 1864, he wrote, "Perhaps Berea is the place where these young colored men now soldiers are to be educated."[15]

A little later that month Fee felt discouraged, because new recruits were not arriving in such numbers as before. "Masters hold on to their slaves as Pharaoh did to his bondmen," Fee explained "The masters now threaten their slaves with what the rebels will do when they come into Ky....Some masters use personal violence; and others offer bribes." But Fee's work continued to be immensely exciting. "Never have I been so intensely interested," he wrote.

> Here are thousands of noble men, made in the image of God, just emerging from the restraints of slavery into the liberties and responsibilities of free men, and of soldiers. I find them manifesting an almost universal desire to learn; and that they do make rapid progress...I feel that it is blessed to labor with such a people....[16]

A "street" in Camp Nelson, 1864. *Courtesy of Berea College Archives/University of Kentucky Photographic Archives*

Fee longed to convince others that the potential he saw in the Negroes could be realized quickly and effectively — that the present generation of ex-slaves was capable of full equality, if people of good will would merely give them initial help. "God by his word and his providence is working glorious changes," Fee said, "The morning light is breaking. May the Christian world be ready for the rapid developments."[17]

The Christian world was not ready, a fact that emerges with tragic clarity in the next months at Camp Nelson and all over the United States. Unfortunately, John G. Fee was unique in his convictions and practice.

In the summer of 1864, Fee had written a proposal to the Secretary of War asking for a government camp for wives of soldiers and other refugees, with the concurrence of Captain Hall, who agreed to set aside 11 square miles of Camp Nelson for such a department. Fee outlined a program by which the Army, with the support of the missionaries, would care for the refugees. In the meantime, Fee had been busy seeking help. Some white men had been stationed at the Camp, and a few volunteer workers had arrived, but their contribution was mostly to add petty jealousies and ambitions to the more serious troubles of the camp. The man most helpful in Fee's work was black, an ex-slave named Gabriel Burdett, who had been a slave preacher at Fork of Dick's River Church in Garrard County before his enlistment. "There is one here of wonderful preaching talent," Fee reported, in one of many letters praising Burdett, "meek, gentle, child-like — I had him detailed for our school work. I teach him."[18]

Fee's concern for Berea continued; however, when he wrote of that place from his station at Camp Nelson, he adopted an objectively critical attitude toward his earlier mission field. "Berea," he noted, "The immediate platt is in a poor region — land poor (most of it) — and the citizens shiftless. Better men can be brought in. The situation is beautiful and very healthful."[19]

At the end of August, 1864, Fee wrote that he was needed in Berea where school was opening. "I must go home and take charge of it unless we can get a male principal. My daughter [Laura] will act as assistant, is now well qualified." He still hoped Partridge would come. Fee himself was torn between Camp Nelson and Berea; close as they were, the road between them was slow-going, and Fee could hardly travel constantly back and forth. "I feel badly about our school at Berea," he confessed, "I told the trustees I thought we could by a vigorous effort have two teachers for the winter term and sustain a good school such as would restore former reputation....This [Camp Nelson] is to me the widest field now. I do not know what it will be ultimately." He felt reluctant to go to Berea at all, because a large number of troops was expected at Camp Nelson just when he was most needed in Berea. He was forced to visit his own home briefly and hurry back to Camp Nelson. "I do not see that I can leave here," he said. "Doors are opening all over the camp for me to preach — this is opening for me a door all over the state where these soldiers (white & black) shall go."[20]

Fee's open-door theory was perfectly correct. For the rest of his life, he was welcomed as a preacher by Kentucky black people. In years to come they would invite him to every corner of the state. Most blacks who first attended Berea went as a result of the great popularity which Fee won at Camp Nelson.

While Berea's school was opening, 1500 new recruits arrived in Camp Nelson, along with many adult females with children. The Berea school enrolled 70 or 80 pupils, no negligible number, but the work at Camp Nelson remained Fee's top priority. "This camp is the finest in our state," Fee said. "Here all the restraints of the slave power are broken. Here are none of the restraints of staid habits. Here is a confluence of minds from East, West, North, South. I am greatly delighted here — because of the open doors...."[21]

Nevertheless, staffing problems at both Camp Nelson and Berea continually harrassed Fee. White workers at the camp quarreled, partly because most of the men wanted the same posts, and they suffered from frequent illnesses. Fee asked the American Missionary Association to give aid to Berea for a principal's salary and received no answer, even though time was running out in his negotiations with Partridge.[22]

Reverend Abisha (or Abishai) Scofield, who with Gabriel Burdett would become one of Fee's most able assistants, arrived at Camp Nelson late in September and immediately began preaching and teaching, as Fee was gone to Berea for the week. Scofield, a native New Yorker, was a seasoned abolitionist and disciple of Gerrit Smith, with whom he had, in 1843, organized the Church of Peterboro, one of the early free churches. Scofield's estimation of the work at Camp Nelson was high: "This school I think is of great importance. The freedmen, children and women too are eager to learn. I have large attentive audiences to preach to, they seem impressable and we can but hope that the seed sown will bring forth good fruit." Scofield's reaction to the whites at Camp Nelson was less sanguine: "I find a number of ministers here," he remarked caustically, "seeking place and pay from the government. As to the labor of preaching they seem quite willing I should do *that*."[23]

Fee remained in Berea for several weeks in August and September, 1864, waiting for Partridge. Meanwhile, he supervised the Berea School himself — his daughter Laura had been hired by the district: 73 students, almost all small children, attended. Eventually, Partridge arrived at Berea to teach, even though Fee had still not heard if the American Missionary Association would supplement the man's salary. Fee wrote repeatedly in fall, 1864, on Partridge's behalf. The former

Oberlin student had gone to Berea on faith, like many before him, assuming he would be supported somehow. As it turned out he was wrong, and so his tenure as a Berea teacher was brief.[24]

Fee was terribly distressed by the lack of money or rather by his inability to pay those to whom he had promised support. He wrote: "I have been very much afflicted with cold and depression of voice. More than in life — I spoke here with hoarseness — rode home — at late hour in night came here very unwell because I had left teachers & others here unpaid." He had had no money from the American Missionary Association during the entire year. In spite of sickness and poverty, he planned to return to Berea the next Sabbath, leaving Scofield in charge of Camp Nelson, and make the journey back and forth "frequently" to "look to the well-being of the work [at Camp Nelson] and at Berea." His own well-being continued to suffer. He fell into a protracted illness which kept him at Berea during the most tragic incident of Camp Nelson's history.[25]

3. The Eviction of Women and Children

Hardships multiplied for Fee and others in the winter of 1864. The white workers at Camp Nelson had been provided with government rations, but Hall — a humane man — was replaced as quartermaster "by an indifferent man," who was unwilling to support the school and who wished to proceed by the letter of the law. He denied rations to Fee and his white helpers, who had to rely upon a newly formed Sanitary Commission for food. Fee was not alone in becoming ill.[26]

Toward the end of November, Fee wrote to the American Missionary Association begging for money. The congregation at Berea had given him less than two dollars since his return; they felt, probably justifiably, that all they could do was care for themselves.[27]

At Camp Nelson matters worsened. Scofield was unable to get wood or stoves for the black people. Soldiers took over the schoolroom, which was converted into a barracks, forcing Scofield to close that school and reduce the number of his pupils to 40, although 200 were eager to attend. With Fee still absent, seriously ill for over a month, and with the replacement of Captain Hall, the one truly sympathetic member of the military staff, no one with power or influence stood between Speed Smith Fry, camp commandant, and the helpless black population under his jurisdiction.

On November 23, 1864, Fry ordered over 400 black women and children turned out of the camp. They were not given time to gather together their few possessions. They were dumped from wagons and carts "in the streets or by the wayside in extreme cold weather." T. E. Hall later reported that "for miles the roads were lined with these poor sufferers." Some froze to death, and all suffered with hunger. One observer saw women and children "lying in barns and mule sheds, wandering through the woods, languishing on the highway."[28]

In an affidavit duly sworn at Camp Nelson December 16, 1864, Reverend Abisha Scofield described the issuing of the order and its immediate aftermath:

> Until the 22nd of last November I never heard any objection made by the military authorities of the Post to the women and children of the colored soldiers residing within the limits of the camp. On Tuesday 22nd of November last the huts and cabins in which the families of the colored soldiers lived ([which had] been erected by the colored soldiers or at the expense of the women) were torn down and the inhabitants were placed in Government wagons and driven outside the lines. The weather at the time was the coldest of the season. The wind was blowing quite sharp and the women and children were thinly clad and mostly without shoes. They were not all driven out on one day but their expulsion occupied about three days.[29]

A slave soldier, Joseph Miller from Lincoln County, related what happened to his wife and four children, aged ten, nine, seven and four. When he enlisted, his master told him to take his wife and children with him because he (the master) would no longer maintain them. Miller reached Camp Nelson with his family, where he put up a tent for them within the camp. One night at six o'clock, the woman and children were told to be gone before early morning. "My little boy," Miller said in his deposition,

> about seven years of age, had been very sick, and was then slowly recovering. My wife had no place to go. I told him [the officer issuing the order] that I was a soldier of the United States. He told me that it did not make any difference: he had orders to take all out of camp. He told my wife and family if they did not get up in the wagon he had, he would shoot the last one of them. On being thus threatened, my wife and children went into the wagon. My wife carried the sick child in her arms. When they left the tent, the wind was blowing hard and cold, and having had to leave much of our clothing when we left our master, my wife, with her little ones, was poorly clad. I followed them as far as the lines. I had had no knowledge where they were taking them. They were in an old meeting-house, belonging to the colored people. The building was very cold, having only one fire. My wife and children could not get

near the fire, because of the numbers of colored people huddling together by the soldiers. I found my wife and family shivering with cold and famished with hunger; they had not received a morsel of food during the whole day. *My boy was dead*. He died directly after getting down from the wagon.[30]

Some women and children were apparently apprehended by former masters, who forced them back into slavery. Scofield stated in a report that "slaveholders [had] been thick around the camp for a few days," indicating his suspicions that General Fry knew why the slaveholders were there.[31]

When Captain Hall returned to Camp Nelson, he was appalled by what he found. Immediately, he telegraphed General Stephen Burbridge, who promptly rescinded Fry's order and sent orders of his own that "all colored women and children seeking refuge in Camp Nelson should be received and cared for."[32]

Scofield immediately set out to find the refugees and restore them to camp. He wrote:

> When they were driven out I had not known where they were to be taken and on the following Sabbath Nov 27 I went in search of the exiles. I found them in Nicholasville about six miles from Camp scattered in various places. Some were in an old store house, some were straying along and lying down in the highway and all appeared to be suffering from exposure to the weather. I gave them some food....the food was absolutely needed. On Monday Nov 28 I saw and conversed with about sixteen women and children who had walked from Nicholasville in the hopes of getting into Camp. The guard refused them admittance. I told the guard that the order by which the women and children were expelled had been countermanded. The guard told me that he had strict orders not to admit them. They were not admitted. Among the number was a young woman who was quite sick and while I was conversing with the guard she lay on the ground. A day or two after this they were allowed to return to camp. They were then very destitute most all complaining of being unwell. Children trembling with cold and wearied with fatigue....[33]

Hall was appointed superintendent and immediately set about constructing necessary buildings — school rooms, workshops — in a section of the camp set aside for them. Fee's proposal for a refugee camp, which had lain dormant for several months, was officially enacted by the Secretary of War. Camp Nelson was now a legal "refuge" for slave women and children related to Union soldiers. This action solved one problem and created a dozen more, but T. E. Hall called it "the deathblow to slavery in Kentucky," probably an accurate estimation. "Had it not been for the inhuman treatment of these poor people," Hall wrote, "we should have had a larger struggle, but great good resulted from the evil."[34]

Although Hall issued orders immediately for the return of the refugees, the struggle with Fry was not over. Fry had Hall arrested and confined to quarters, not to communicate with any headquarters but his own. Hall shrewdly ignored his superior and sent a dispatch to Brigadier General Thomas, securing his own release in less than eight hours. Then Fry received orders relieving him of his command.[35]

It was easier to order the return of the people evicted from the camp than to achieve it. Some came back of their own accord in groups of two to twenty at a time, having suffered incredible hardships: "some of them [had] lain down and died by the way." Some, as we have seen, had been taken back into slavery. Scofield, writing in December, recorded his determination to find those victims and secure their deliverance. He and John Vetters, another camp worker, spent two weeks doing little but caring for returning Negroes. "They are crowded together in our school room," Scofield reported, "sick and dying. We draw rations for them and feed them. For half a day at a time we stand in the cold, call over their names and deal out bread and meat to 350 poor hungry creatures."[36]

Captain Hall planned for large and suitable buildings, but they had to be constructed, and that took precious time. Scofield's own wife, living in New York with a large family of children, wrote him that she was out of money and provisions, and soon he himself became ill.[37]

Hall applied to the American Missionary Association for help: "What can you do for the poor in this camp?" he asked, "Remember they come here destitute of everything." In December, Vetters reported that he had found one child about two years old entirely naked. "It had not one thread of clothing and her mother could not get out of bed for want of clothes."[38]

At the first of January, 1865, Fee, not entirely well himself, returned to Camp Nelson, where he found great suffering. "The faith of the soldiers," he wrote, "had been greatly injured by the Army's callous disregard of their families." However, he was happy that his request for refugees had been granted, and he foresaw that work at Camp Nelson would increase. In fact, the expulsion gave impetus to the passage of Fee's proposal.[39]

Of 400 people sent out of Camp Nelson in November, 1864, 250 returned, but 102 of them died afterwards. By the time of Fee's return in January, 1865, women and children were coming in "by dozens at a time." Eventually, "Camp Nelson became a refuge for three thousand sixty slaves, mostly women and children." Hall reported (June, 1865):

> Not a day passes during which I am not entreated by some poor defenceless wife or child to interfere for their protection against the fury of their master....Only this day, a colored woman walked from Nicholasville six miles, bringing in her arms the *body of her dead child* because the Chivalry in Nicholasville through prejiduce [sic] refused it burial![40]

By January 2, 1865, Fee had received necessary authorization to admit women and children to an official refugee camp, and by January 10, he was contacted by General Burbridge, who told him that Fee's paper to the Secretary of War had been sent back to Burbridge for approval. And he did approve — "with all his heart." "He offered me facilities [for the women and children]," Fee wrote, "God opens the way."[41]

Despite the new order at Camp Nelson, trouble constantly erupted from tensions between workers. Hall and Fee disagreed about who should be camp superintendent: Hall wanted Reverend Lester Williams, and Fee held out for Reverend Abisha Scofield. Hall won.

On January 20, when Fee was gone to Berea for another brief visit, Gabriel Burdett wrote for advice. "Some things do not please me," he stated, "for I love peace and union and I have lived long enough to know that if men do not love each other they do not love God...." Disagreements and strife among the white staff continued constantly for months. So did deaths among the black population. Burdett reported on January 20, "There has been much sickness and many deaths here. Since Dec 24th/64, there has been 43 deaths and still they die."[42]

Fee, back in Camp Nelson, found Superintendent Lester Williams inadequate in many respects. "Bro Williams," he stated, "may do better soon as weather grows warmer and he will not be spattered with mud, but bandbox Christians do not suffice for the rough & tumble of camp life & a people who need to be gathered up into the arms of love & pulled out of the mire & filth of sin & suffering." Scofield, on the other hand, worked long and hard for the people. In January, he traveled North to get clothing for the naked women and children (he went to Syracuse, Lebanon, Georgetown, Hamilton and Peterboro in New York). In Cincinnati, he found blankets and a stove. By February 4, he was back in camp "dealing the stuff out." Fee urged Scofield to bring his family to Camp Nelson, but he simply could not afford to do so.[43]

Fee wrote disapprovingly of Williams' "down Eastern" manner of preaching, which was, Fee said, no good for freedmen. Williams was not accustomed to manual labor, as Scofield was; Fee thought Scofield would be altogether better as superintendent than Williams, but to no avail. Williams laid plans to bring his wife to the camp as teacher, and if Reverend Williams was unsatisfactory, Mrs. Williams was to prove simply impossible.

In spite of staff difficulties, Fee moved forward theoretically and practically in the Camp Nelson work. "This much is certain," he wrote George Whipple, "much of the instruction to this people must be oral. This has been habit of life transmitted to the children, kind social mingling with example that their imitation can take hold of — presentation of truth, principle in conformity to their habits." Fee's theory of the proper mode of education for ex-slaves scarcely seems revolutionary, but simple and obvious as it was, it occurred to few white educators after the Civil War.[44]

On the practical end, Fee objected to some of Hall's building plans. Hall proposed and erected an enormous bunkhouse for 125 women and children. "125 persons in a continuous babel," Fee complained, "children crying, mothers fretting." He wanted money spent on little cottages for eight or ten persons at the most.[45]

Early in 1865, Fee had a chance to become general superintendent of camp, but he refused, because he wanted to go on preaching; he felt also that he could not accept the post because of his obligation to his own children in Berea.[46]

Fee's knowledge of slavery, now that the system was virtually dead, had become more intimate. Southerners still, and for years to come, defended their peculiar institution. From the experiences of Camp Nelson, Fee drew his final conclusions about slavery and about equality. Nothing on earth could convince him that slavery was justified. Nothing could convince him that any system but total, unqualified equality was just.

> I know one of our representatives in congress said a few days since that 'slavery in Ky was not that horrible thing which northern abolitionists describe' — Slavery is essentially the same everywhere — it is a system of force and violence. As counted a few days since there were within this camp, seven hundred and fifty three women and children. Of this number one hundred and fifty say they were cruelly treated on account of their husband's enlisting, and three hundred and ten say they were driven off from home. There were [some] so horribly lacerated that the military authorities after examinations by surgeons sent them to Cincinnati....Of the first three thousand colored men examined in this camp for military service three out of five bore on their bodies marks of

Camp Nelson refugees instructed by an American Missionary Association teacher, with supervisor watching, 1864.
Courtesy of Berea College Archives/University of Kentucky Photographic Archives

cruelty. This is to me the personal statement of both the surgeons who examined them.

Many of these women & children have not enough of one poor dirty suit to cover them well — no changes of raiment.

No class of people on this earth are to me more hopeful, so far as moral good is concerned than these ex-slaves of Kentucky — so receptive, obedient, trusting. We ought to praise God for this free access to these humble, trusting millions. Tis a privilege to give and be co-workers with Christ in the redemption of suffering humanity.[47]

After Hall was appointed general superintendent for the whole camp, Fee expressed his desire to settle either at Berea or Camp Nelson with his family — but his strongest inclination was toward Camp Nelson. "I have great sympathy for these colored people," he wrote, "tis meat & drink to me to help them & in God's providence I know the anti-slavery enterprise & habits of this people better than I do science." Fee had been made an expert, not by study and investigation, but by love. His desire for justice for blacks sprang from his ardent and genuine affection for them — no cold abstractions for Fee. The cause of the slaves was for him a burning passion. To the end of his life he was on fire with zeal for a cause: genuine equality for every person. But his great cause never became a lofty overgeneralization. It always appeared incarnate in his love for the actual, individual black people with whom he lived and worked.[48]

At the end of February, 1865, Fee acknowledged a gift of money from the American Missionary Association; he had spent it on clothing and shoes for the women and children of Camp Nelson:

There was at time of your gift cold, wet, snowy weather. Many had not shoes or stockings — others had not a change of under garments, nor enough to keep them warm....The first benefaction was to an aged colored woman who had in the army *five* sons — her husband a few years since was whipped to death in Fayette co., Ky. — The mother is feeble with neuralgia — is very neat in person; and previous to the cruel exposure, in throwing them out of camp, was paying her rent — sustaining herself by washing & sewing, laid up some seven dollars. This was all expended when your favor came.

There is yet much distress & mortality....The buildings now prepared, though somewhat artistic & well-*meant* are not suitable for women and children. With 150 persons in one building — noise, disease & death rage — Oh, the suffering incident to slavery! Today as I looked upon the sick and dead — little ones — I was completely overcome & wept for the poor sufferers.[49]

But on February 15, 1865, James Brisbin wrote Fee that no additional homes could be erected and no more women and children encouraged to come. "Only those who are ill-treated and indigent should be received, only the worst cases should be received."

"The poor creatures need someone who will mingle among them," Fee wrote; he was still laboring to have the ward system abolished, to put his cottage-plan into action. "Cottages are cheaper in erection than wards," he said,

> it is cheaper to buy additional wood than coffins and graves. The habits of this people must be considered. They have been *accustomed* to the fireplace & cabin....How blessed the gospel of Christ that teaches us to bear one another's burdens. I now expect to spend days & perhaps weeks here in helping to relieve suffering & trying to make *freedom a success*. If the effort *here* fails this will hinder the cause of freedom all over the state.[50]

In spite of disagreements, Hall continued to help Fee, who perceived that the captain had "sympathy for the poor & quick perceptions of the right." (Fee could not forbear, however, remarking that Hall liked his "*dram*.") Hall consented to Fee's cottage plan, on the condition that colored soldiers pay for houses erected for their families, with the government supplying the lumber. After all, Hall said, "white soldiers support their own families."[51]

Infant mortality was terrible in the camp, particularly in the wards Fee found so objectionable. "Four deaths last night," he recorded, "four night before." His assistants were fixing bunks, finding better bread and fruit to give the sick a change of diet and bathing patients.[52]

Fee's son Burritt was with him at Camp Nelson during February. Only 15, Burritt had already taught at Berea, and Scofield wanted his help at Camp Nelson in teaching the soldiers (male and female schools were separate). Fee decided to leave his son at the camp for a month, but within a few days the young man was so sick that Fee considered taking him home to Berea. (This illness seems the first in a long series which led to Burritt's early death.) On February 25, 1865, when Burritt was very ill, Fee wrote:

> This is a turning point — a crisis in our history here...We had a case yesterday that was a sort of test question. A slaveholder, a 'good Union man' wife a New York woman called to get a slave girl. Capt. Hall said, "Yes — I know

Mr. Barnes she will be better off than here." Bro. Williams said "No." I said *No*! The Captain gave me a private chat. I said, "No! — not for a moment!! 1 Her *father* is here a soldier — natural guardian. 2 We must do for her *morally* what Mr. Barnes as a *chattel* owner will not do — this is more than "hog & hominy." 3 I said we have the right on our side — with it the letter of the law — war department, on our side this time, and we will use the opportunity to 'knock the starch' out of slavery far as we can — tis slavery that stands between Ky & loyalty — tis these respectable slave holders that makes [sic] the institution tolerable. The Capt winced & retired.[53]

Fee's defence of the girl threatened with re-enslavement was paralleled months later by his campaign for equal treatment for a black teacher. In the direct involvement and confrontations of Camp Nelson, Fee found his most satisfying and demanding work. "If I were not connected with the Berea School I should pitch my tent here," he said, "and link my future with these colored people...." As it turned out, he would pitch his tent in Berea and still link his life with these same black people.[54]

A new boy in Camp Nelson, shining a pair of boots for a government official, was asked, "You black boots! What did you come to Camp Nelson for?"

"I come for liberty," he replied, "Ain't that enough?" Then he added, "I come to learn too."[55]

4. Contrabands and Administrators

The War Between the States ended in April, 1865, but the new conditions it had created would present problems for years. In Camp Nelson some of the most pressing needs of the black population were met: better shelters had been erected, schools were operating, religious services were frequent and well-attended. The greatest continuing difficulty at the camp involved the white people, not the blacks. Problems of staffing occurred constantly: many workers were laboring under the auspices of the American Missionary Association, although the Army continued to regulate the camp — with Freedmen's Bureau and Sanitary Commission also in the picture. Authority and hierarchy in the various organizations created administrative muddles. But the group of non-military white workers was so small that simple personality clashes between individuals created hardships for hundreds of people (especially black ones) in the camp.

Rivalry between workers led to dissension. In March, 1865, Scofield returned to camp after a visit to his home and discovered that Captain Hall had given Scofield's job to Lester Williams. Scofield felt Hall and his friends had taken control simply in expectation of large government salaries. Williams himself had expressed himself "heartily sick of [camp life]" and was expected to leave momentarily, along with Vetters, his clerk.[56]

Fee maintained his own position, which was so nearly unofficial that he was somehow immune from most administrative disasters. He continued to minister to the sick, helped with the management of the fugitive home, aided in refitting the schoolroom for the soldiers, being taught at this point by Burritt Fee and Gabriel Burdett, with Scofield superintending. Fee also preached to three regiments of colored troops. But he was unable to devote himself to preaching as he thought he should. He had been offered the superintendency of the camp and debated whether to take it.[57]

Williams, after a brief disagreement with Hall, went to Cincinnati to fetch his wife, slated as a new teacher for the women and children. Hall, who owned an oil company, was expected to quit his post at the camp soon to look after business interests.[58]

Fee was forced to keep riding back and forth between the camp and Berea, where his wife was suffering an unusually difficult pregnancy before the birth of their last child (Elizabeth Hamilton "Bessie" Fee, born April, 1865). "I am interested in the work here yet the majority are women and children — soldiers enough now to preach to — don't know how long they will stay." In April, 1865, Camp Nelson had a population of 1,500-1,600 women, with 1,000 waiting to get in and 6,000 expected to arrive at some indefinite time.[59]

Plans were made for the Berea project to start up in full force. By April 14, 1865, John A. R. Rogers, Berea's most important teacher before the war, had finished arrangements to move back from Ohio. Fee was juggling numerous responsibilities. On April 21, when Elnathan Davis arrived to serve as American Missionary Association agent at Camp Nelson, Fee planned to go to Berea to a trustee's meeting on the following day.[60]

Even before Davis' arrival, Fee felt that Camp Nelson had too much overseeing — virtually every white person in camp insisted on overseeing something. The accounts become confusing, since four or five people may all be "superintendent" in some guise simultaneously — superintendent of the whole camp, superintendent of the men's school, superintendent of the women's school, superintendent of the teachers, superintendent of the women, etc. The reason for this proliferation of authoritative titles and roles is not far to seek: the small group of whites "overseeing" the large group of blacks felt it necessary to develop and maintain a caste system as their surest defense against the new racial threat: equality. The development of authority, officialdom and red tape was swift and sure. Through rules, regulations, restrictions and institutionalized rigidity, whites at Camp Nelson apparently hoped (whether consciously or not) to keep their black charges safely subordinate. The system began as "administration" but soon stood revealed as overt racism. Fee's unwillingness to assume the role of superintendent, even though he worked harder than anyone else in camp, is characteristic. Of all the Camp Nelson workers, he was the only one willing to forego authority and approach the work with simple humanity.

Fee began to sense the problem long before it emerged in its naked ugliness. In May, he wrote:

> I will speak this once. The men and women who will be appropriate helpers for this people must be those [who] can mingle amongst them & treat them *kindly*.
>
> But if a superintendent or teacher is reserved & cross if when one trembling fugitive comes into his presence and begins to enquire and he gruffly says "Who are you" I am Milly. They tell me there is a letter here for me — "They tell many stories about letters." The woman retires. This [is?] all.

By this time the white people of Camp Nelson were not attending Fee's preaching anymore — a mere hint of the hostility forming against him.[61]

Fee differed strongly with others about the kind of workers the camp needed. He wished for some helpers he had known in the past. "Bro Candee's wife," he wrote, "would be to these people worth all the women we have here....Bro. Davis and Capt Hall think we need 'Massachusetts precision' here in Ky.," Fee stated, "no doubt. But these poor babes need not starch and fastidiousness but Christ like simplicity." Fee had told Elnathan Davis, who was to be in charge of American Missionary Association selections for Camp Nelson posts, that the camp needed "that easy frank active simple piety that [had] so often attended the Oberlin school and Western man rather than 'Massachusetts precision.'"[62]

In the same letter, Fee mentioned John A. R. Rogers, evidently connecting him with the Oberlin qualifications he had enumerated. "Berea has a *principle*," Fee said, "worth making an effort for — it must go forward." He was very conscious of the effort Berea required, since he himself was so deeply involved in Camp Nelson that every duty to Berea cost him much more time and energy than ever before.[63]

His campaign for Oberlin teachers at Camp Nelson eventually bore fruit when Willard Watson Wheeler and his wife Ellen arrived in the summer, but in the meantime the American Missionary Association commissioned Gabriel Burdett, still a Union soldier, to preach and teach at Camp Nelson. The diverse demands upon Fee at this time are revealed in his statement (May 18, 1865) that he needed to find a stove for Gabriel Burdett, and he thought the prospect was good for getting a charter for Berea. This distracting combination of priorities appears again and again in Fee's letters of the period.[64]

Almost as soon as Ann E. W. Williams (wife of Reverend Lester Williams) arrived, she became superintendent of the school for women and children, a project Fee had been involved with from the first. He had developed his own theories about how the work should be conducted, which would not square with her views. "We ought to have here some colored teachers: 1. That these people may *see* what they *can* be. 2. That by *example* we may help put down the spirit of cast." By this time, Fee had ample opportunity to see that the spirit of caste would not disappear with the abolition of slavery. Another racist attitude was coming into prominence — the attitude that had once taken the form of colonization proposals, plans formulated by white people for the removal and/or "disposal" of black people. Fee wrote:

> It is not as I believe best to move the colored people from this state. Some favor this. 1. They ought for highest good to have homes of their own — better than to be floating hirelings, better for their children also, *parents* can watch over them. 2. Lands here are cheaper than in free states. 3. The presence of free people of color will help continue the weakness of slavery — until *all* hope is gone of its recuperation. 4. Climate here suits these colored people.[65]

Captain Hall wanted to send all Camp Nelson blacks to free states in colonies by themselves; Fee objected to both ideas — he was in favor of having blacks and whites living interspersed together, and he maintained that ex-slaves of Kentucky had a right to live in Kentucky if they wished.

In addition, he pointed out, "This is just what the slave owners want — absence of 'free niggers' [slavery existed legally in Kentucky until December 6, 1865] — then what they have are more quiet & secure."[66] Fee wrote:

> I have a discussion going on in my own mind. Camp Nelson cannot be the receptacle for *all*. How then shall we get education to the great mass who stay scattered over the country. What we have here is only a drop in the buckett [sic].
>
> Outside of military posts the people will not yet be favorable to schools where colored children can be taught. We think we can do this at Berea soon as we can ready for the children — next Spring. Get house up this fall & winter.[67]

Clearly, in Fee's thinking the problem of Camp Nelson and the solution of Berea were coming closer and closer to juxtaposition. Fee eventually believed Berea College would function as *the* school where the people of Camp Nelson would be educated, along with an indigenous white population.

In a letter to the American Missionary Association, May 30, 1865, Fee described his own internal debate about Berea and Camp Nelson. He headed the passage with the word "Decision" underlined twice. "Is it best," he asked, "to get colored children & whites into the same towns and schools or will that be all the while a forced effort and small and we be compelled to get the colored people together in groups for a generation and there educate and then by the force of example in persons already educated & cultivated break down the spirit of cast?"[68]

In a way, Fee's final decision was to opt for both propositions. At Camp Nelson he would attempt to maintain a colony and school of black people living together, but at Berea he would bring together black and white people in the same small town and school. The white constituency for Berea's unique educational and social experiment would be drawn from the mountains, where slavery had never been powerfully entrenched; the black constituency would be drawn mainly from the soldiers and refugees of Camp Nelson.

In the months immediately following the close of the war, Camp Nelson was a very unstable settlement. Personnel changes occurred fairly constantly: Gabriel Burdett, for example, was called to his regiment in May, to be sent to Texas; policies about ex-slaves and those slaves still held in bondage in Kentucky were in constant flux. The staff assembled at Camp Nelson included individuals Fee thought inadequate to the task.

Teachers were badly needed: the camp had schoolrooms ready for five hundred people in May, 1865, when the staff was simply too small to cope with such numbers of students. Fee expressed his unhappiness with Mrs. Williams, whose penchant was for much "organizing." Fee felt he bore the responsibility for the defective work — he knew exactly what was required: a kind of "Christianity that can take [the poor] to his table, *work* with them, and show by example — in marked patience & kindness bear their infirmities." But it was one thing to know what was required, quite another to find people who could live up to such ideals of Christian behavior. Too often at Camp Nelson, Fee observed the "finely dressed gentleman with his hands in his pockets, only to give orders." In strong protest, he wrote, "The sub-assistants should not be fashionable young men on horseback to drive women & children after the 'plantation' order."[69]

Scofield worked well as a teacher but suffered from jealousy of the usurping Reverend Williams and Williams' side-kick, Vetters. Fee also strongly objected to Williams.[70]

The camp remained painfully understaffed. Fee noted with asperity that Williams was sick but would not *teach* if well. In an attempt to establish a Sabbath School, Fee gathered together 527 children between the ages of five and twenty, six of whom could read. He had nobody to help him save Mrs. Caroline Daimon, a widowed friend of Captain Hall, hired on Hall's recommendation.[71]

Fee's Camp Nelson work complicated his efforts to deal with Berea and with larger issues as well, but he never dropped one responsibility simply because he had picked up another. In May, 1865, he worked to get rebel land confiscated and sold to blacks and find a tenth trustee to sign Berea's charter. During this whole period of his life, Fee's specific labors, for two very demanding and frustrating enterprises, were accompanied by much thought and writing about general solutions to the racial problem. Certainly few white men could better know the ins and outs of the black situation in Kentucky than Fee.

Even though the war was over, Fee observed "the habit of slavery lives yet." In fact, the habit of slavery continued in both black and white, Camp Nelson being a case in point, with its authoritarian hierarchies: the militant white command over the servile and helpless former slaves. Fee's recommendation dealt with both these impediments to progress: "We need now," he wrote,

> to remove fast as possible all unnatural appliances [the regulations of camp life] and restore those of compensation and natural affection — we need to get these people in cottages attached to *small plots* of *ground* or some mechanical labor from either or both of which they can *earn* something. They will work for *themselves* as they will not for Uncle Sam or any other than self. In doing so they will *govern themselves* thus far and avoid the *driving* of *overseers.*

In this passage Fee demonstrates his awareness that the spectre of slavery still hovered over the relationship between black and white. Slavery could be reinstated quite easily under another name. He saw the need for black autonomy, self-government, as soon as possible, to avoid permanent white overlords. After all, most black people had simply moved from one form of bondage to another — the salient feature of Camp Nelson was certainly not *freedom.*[72]

Fee visited more than 100 black families, in all about 1,000 people, during this period, interviewing each individual concerning her or his domestic, social and religious state. His findings convinced him of the importance of obtaining land for them to purchase and machinery so they could begin to work "remuneratively."

"Also," he wrote,

> Let those who are appointed to instruct be men and women *eminently Christian* — not with morality — mere uprightness — but with *Christlike sympathy*. There must be a *personal* influence *with* these people continually — a person or persons who, whilst he does not condescend to any vileness or trifling, yet does not hold these people at arms length with the idea that dignity and reservation is power — *confidence and affection* is.[73]

Unlike those of many white contemporaries, Fee's goals for the black people never included putting them down into a new subordinate role. He sought to help them reach their own "self-sufficiency" through every means in his power. He felt the division of his efforts between Camp Nelson and Berea hindered his effectiveness, however, and he longed to pursue his work for the Negroes definitely at one place or the other. Again and again, he weighed and compared the two possible institutions: Camp Nelson had coal, Berea had timber; Camp Nelson had a more immediately needy population, Berea had a heritage of principles; Camp Nelson held out little possibility for interracial education, while Berea, with its white citizens already interested in the school, seemed promising in that respect.[74]

In either case, Camp Nelson or Berea, Fee saw clearly what risks lay ahead. "There is danger just here," he wrote,

> that after all we are attempting to treat the black man as a 'nigger' not as other men — To get the right use of his bones and muscles he must stand as other men — not too much nursing. Also we should avoid making a 'nigger school' — avoid the idea that there must be separation. I believe we ought to make this a school for humanity — make efforts to have in here a due measure of white faces. I fear we shall not able to get this here [in Camp Nelson]. Already the impression with all classes is that this camp is for black people. We may have to make the true model at Berea — probably try at both.

The question occupied Fee's mind for weeks: he asked George Whipple, Corresponding Secretary of the American Missionary Association, his opinion about the probability of success with a school for colored and white. Fee's own opinion, emerging more and more clearly, was that such an enterprise could succeed. He believed the gospel and the war together were fast overcoming prejudice. He asked Whipple's opinion also about the feasibility of having whites and blacks living interspersed all over the country, but Fee had already decided that interspersion was the answer to the racial problem, partly because only by living near sympathetic whites could blacks hope to procure land. In addition, Fee always believed racial prejudice could be overcome by actual knowledge. His own experience stood as a model for him; his love for black people resulted from his knowing them very well. He did not stand aloof from them; through living with them, he had come to respect and esteem them. His expectation was that other people would respond the same way — only actual contact could overcome prejudice.[75]

In June, 1865, Scofield visited Berea, since he was considering moving there to become a resident trustee if Fee decided to make Berea College his permanent work. Scofield liked what he saw there, acknowledging after his visit that Fee's desire to maintain his hold in Berea was just. On his return to Camp Nelson, Scofield found Fee much dissatisfied with the management of the Refugee home, which he considered altogether too "stiff and warlike for such an enterprise." Scofield thought the Camp Nelson problem was unique, since it was the only military camp in the country which was for women and children as well as for men; it was also a camp in a state of peace rather than war. Unfortunately, these distinctions failed to penetrate the rhinoceros hide of the administrative mind. The women and children at Camp Nelson were being given soldiers' rations and fare, and guards and whips and bullets were "made fearfully imposing."[76]

On June 15, 1865, Scofield filed an appalling report:

> If you want facts you can have them. The mortality here is fearful. From one sixth to one seventh of the whole number die every month! They come and die! Come and die! This results from two causes, 1st bad plan, 2nd bad management. It is a bad plan — to crowd so many of these poor people together. It makes a great show but there is 'death in the pot.' It will never do! [About 1200 people had died in camp within the year.]
>
> 2nd. It is bad to have a dozen men and women to care for these poor men who [are] rarely much with them — never know their wants — till they are dead — *bad* to feed sick children on ham — bad to let sick women lie on bare boards — when the straw lies unused under the shed.[77]

The school was doing very little, Scofield said, because Mrs. Williams, the new superintendent, was feeble and "unable to go forward with such heavy work." Fee and Scofield offered to do the work, but she told them it was none of their business.[78]

By June 27, 1865, Fee had organized a class for boys at Camp Nelson and left Scofield in charge, but Reverend Lester Williams stopped it. Mrs. Daimon had one class for girls. Williams and his wife were directly opposing Fee and his friends — as later events would reveal, the Williams couple found their primary motivation in hatred for Fee and gave more time and energy to thwarting his plans than in aiding the black people in their charge.

Fee reported on the situation to the American Missionary Association: "The people continue to die in a ratio terrible at rate of 190 per month out of a population of near twenty two hundred." Most cottages were without stoves or fireplaces; each house contained eight to twelve people in one room 16 feet square. Each shelter had only one door, because Hall had refused to include a back door with a place for a wash-shed. Fee had proposed such a plan — logically enough — but Hall had rejected it on the grounds that it was not "artistic" (i.e., would lead to messy backyards). In utter frustration, Fee wrote that this situation had to be changed or he would go home to Berea to "link [himself] with a growing enterprise — rather than a dying one."[79]

On a more hopeful note, he said preparations were being made for a Fourth of July such as Kentucky had never witnessed. At Camp Nelson, from five to ten thousand black people were expected, coming from the countryside in a radius of 20 miles. They would have cannon, drums, fifes, dinner, amusements. Fee described this extraordinary celebration for the *Louisville Union* (July 7, 1865) — he had been ailing during the festivities, but his account is nothing if not enthusiastic. The day began with a grand military review, then the women, "who had been free for fewer than six months, set up tables and brought out bread, meat and pies that they had been preparing." The soldiers, women and children gathered then at the speakers' platform, where a soldier offered a prayer, the schoolchildren sang songs, a non-commissioned officer read the Declaration of Independence, a sergeant and another black soldier spoke. (There were no white speakers.) Finally, to the sound of martial music, the crowd retired to the picnic tables. The celebration had included no drunks, no rows, no arrests — it was more orderly, Fee said, than a white gathering of equal numbers. Fee estimated that "5 to 7 thousand colored people [were] present" at this event.[80]

Fee cannot have enjoyed this celebration much personally, however, because before the Fourth, he had become violently ill with diarrhea, an affliction which had worsened by July 6. Others also became ill, Mrs. Williams, for example — or remained so: Mrs. Daimon was quite sick and had not been in the school one week since her arrival and was planning to return to Massachusetts within the week (she did not go). In his illness, Fee grew desperate about his circumstances: "I must have my family here or go & stay with them," he wrote. Camp Nelson had no facilities for them; the whole situation put him in a terrible quandary.[81]

On July 11, 1865, General John M. Palmer issued an order that made it possible for black people to move freely about the state and seek employment on their own: a kind of perpetual pass to all. This new possibility was bound to change the Camp Nelson situation. Meantime, without having sought the post, Fee found himself appointed, by General Clinton B. Fisk, new superintendent of Camp Nelson. Fee had told the General that he (Fee) could not stay at Camp Nelson unless there was a prospect of having a continued school in which to "*train youth*." Some 3,000 soldiers had been stationed at the camp by this time, changing the population again (at times it had been almost wholly peopled by women and children, at other times almost wholly by soldiers or training recruits). These men clamored for teaching and preaching — Scofield did what he could, and Fee helped as much as possible, taking time from his new duties as superintendent of the Refugee Home.[82]

Fee's new role as administrator was not to his taste and must have been a burden rather than a privilege; he longed to be with his family permanently, but the camp was not as good a place for his sons as Berea, as far as Fee was concerned, and he still had no residence for his family. General Fisk thought the American Missionary Association should pay for a house for the Fees at Camp Nelson (apparently, the American Missionary Association did not share this opinion). In addition, Fee had developed grave doubts about the military regimen, wondering if army control established the best circumstances for a school. Once again he wrote, "It may be that Berea will be found to be the best place for this school. This one cannot be removed for the present and I think it will continue here."[83]

Fee recommended that the American Missionary Association hire an agent to find employment for black people who were "strangers to the country." Their limited experience as slaves and, in the case of the men, as soldiers, did not equip them to move out into the world. They had neither money nor — quite understandably — courage for such a journey.[84]

By late summer, 1865, new staff members arrived at the camp: Willard Watson Wheeler and his wife Ellen; Wheeler, an Oberlin graduate, had served in the Union Army but had been captured and spent most of the war in Confederate prisons. As a result, he was in very poor health — as it turned out, permanently. But Fee greeted his arrival with enthusiasm, recommended him as principal in the refugee school.[85]

The next stage of Camp Nelson experience began when Clinton B. Fisk wrote to Fee on August 4, 1865, saying, "My positive instructions from Washington are 'to break up the Refugee Home at Camp Nelson at the earliest possible day consistent with humanity & c.' This cannot be done immediately but we must not make any more with a few [view?] to permanency there. Yourself and friends ought to carry out your old scheme of permanent industrial school at your old home. Private enterprise and benevolence must look to the elevation of the race." Fisk added this commendation: "I wish I had a hundred John G. Fees."[86]

Others did not share Fisk's view. Reverend Lester Williams in particular found even one John G. Fee far too many. In August, 1865, he wrote to Michael E. Strieby of the American Missionary Association to complain that Fee was a "singularly unfortunate" choice to represent the Association at Camp Nelson. Williams claimed that Fee's fellow-workers did not respect him and placed no confidence in him. Fee was "restless, uneasy," interfering, "double-minded, double-tongued, [and] double-dealing." Williams concluded his diatribe by asking if Fee was insane.[87]

The strife among Camp Nelson workers was moving toward a crisis. Ironically, Fee wrote a letter to Strieby on August 11, too — his report on the same day strikes quite a different note from Williams'. Fee stated that Camp Nelson would prove to be hard to break up. Probably a town would form there when the military had withdrawn. For himself, he mentioned two invitations he had received to address black people (former Camp Nelson residents) now living as freedmen in Lexington and Danville. They had asked him to organize schools and procure aid for them, and he planned to comply with their requests.[88]

The first outbreak of open hostility among Camp Nelson staff came in August, an incident small compared to what would follow. By August 16, Captain Hall had left the camp permanently and one Colonel Bierbower, a man of very different habits, replaced him. Bierbower, Fee wrote, "does not realize the necessity of having spiritually minded teachers — loves wom[en] wine and music." Bierbower kept late hours and enjoyed partying. One Wednesday night in August, he procured the services of a violinist and gathered some staff together, whereupon one of the men, the undertaker in camp, asked a teacher (sent by the Freedmen Aid Society) to waltz with him.

A new staff member, Mrs. Mary Colton, nee Thome (sister of Lane Rebel James A. Thome, and herself an early student at Oberlin College), heard the music and dancing and assumed that "the colored people had possession of the room below." Annoyed, she got up to ask them to go away — seeing "whites," she turned in disgust and flew to Fee's room where she woke him up and "asked if such things were to be allowed here." He "cried out not if I were superintendent." The next day, Mrs. Colton at the breakfast table talked to Mrs. Daimon in "a manner abrupt & severe," informed her that other young ladies of "exemplary" behavior wanted to work at Camp Nelson, and that she (Mrs. Colton) was writing a report about the proceedings.[89]

Eventually Mrs. Colton apologized to Mrs. Daimon for her severe manner, but the young white ladies in the camp would not be reconciled to the interfering widow. Colonel Bierbower was "lugged into [the affair]" and displayed his chivalry for the young women by getting up an order suggested by Reverend Williams and written up by Mrs. Williams, to send Mrs. Colton out of camp. "This was to me a great trial," Fee wrote. He felt Mrs. Colton had been treated unfairly, even though he regretted her manner and speech.[90]

Fee concluded from this teapot tempest that the men in the camp were a hindrance to Christ's work and expressed his intention to root them out. "Sad it is," he wrote, "to have these poor creatures (ex-slaves) turn away in disgust from their professed friends." Clearly the dancing incident won no friends for Fee and no supporters for his projects. While the incident appears comically petty, with a degree of absurdity no one would dare invent, it nourished an enmity to Fee which had been growing more or less secretly. He was surrounded by racists who hated everything he stood for. Like many of Fee's later enemies, the Camp Nelson faction was pleased to catch him in narrow, "fanatical" behavior, because John G. Fee had to be discredited at all costs. His views on dancing, for example, made it easier to "prove" that his views on human equality were erroneous — how could such a narrow-minded man see the racial issue clearly?[91]

Apparently ignorant of the difficulty looming at Camp Nelson, Fee continued to report the problems and achievements of Berea. On August 22, he wrote that John A. R. Rogers had agreed to go to Berea in the spring, while John G. Hanson had resettled there. Both whites and blacks were gathering at Berea in preparation for work to resume.[92]

Willard W. Wheeler and Ellen P. T. Wheeler — workers from Camp Nelson who became teachers at Berea in 1865.

Courtesy of Berea College Archives

5. The Belle Mitchell Incident

Meanwhile, the final controversy of Fee's Camp Nelson was developing apace. When he visited Danville at the invitation of black people who had asked help in setting up schools, he met a young woman, almost white but of black ancestry, and hired her to teach at Camp Nelson. She was described as being virtually European in appearance, with straight hair and very light skin. Nevertheless, according to traditions of white America, she was black. Her name was Belle Mitchell; she had studied to be a teacher at Xenia, Ohio, though when she arrived at Camp Nelson she was only 18 years old.[93]

In his *History of Berea*, Fee narrates the story of his meeting with Belle Mitchell. On

> a Sabbath in a neighboring city, I saw in the congregation (colored) a young woman of light complexion, whose manner, as she came to the altar to partake of the Lord's Supper, favorably impressed me. I enquired of the pastor who she was. He told me she was a member of that church, with fair education and good parentage. Immediately it occurred to me that she was the woman with whom to test the caste question among the teachers at Camp Nelson, and set the precedent of giving positions to colored persons as fast as prepared for such. Monday morning I called on her parents and told them my wish and plan. I also suggested to them and the daughter what might be the opposition, but such, I said, would be un-Christ-like, and the sooner met the better, and that perhaps the daughter was 'raised up for a time like this.'[94]

Belle's parents consented to the arrangement, and the young woman arrived at Camp Nelson, where Fee assigned her a room in the dormitory and put her in charge of a class of pupils. "At the dinner hour," he writes,

> I gave to her in the common dining-hall a chair and place at the table at which I presided. The presence of this young lady at one of the several tables in the common dining-hall produced a sensation. A chaplain to one of the regiments, whose home was down in Maine [Chapin], together with some army officials also boarding at the hall, protested against this young woman's eating in the common boarding-hall. All the lady teachers (white) sent there by the American Missionary Association and the Freedman's Aid Society, refused, with two exceptions [Mrs. Colton

and her daughter Anna Smith], to come to the first tables whilst the young woman was eating....

A Major, whose home was in Illinois, and the steward, whose home was in the same state, came to me and suggested that I remove the young woman. I saw the moment for decision had come and in a quiet manner said "I will suffer my right arm torn from my body before I will remove the young woman." And that they might see that I was not arbitrary in my decision, I said, "The young woman is fitted for her position, is modest and discreet, she is a Christian and as such Christ's representative. What I do to her, I do to him." Both of these men were professing Christians, and one of them a local preacher at home.

The steward said his wife would not give to the young woman a plate. I replied, "Then she shall have mine, and I will have another:" for the control had been given to me, and I meant to keep it to use it.[95]

Thus Fee's test on the caste-issue with the Camp Nelson staff resulted in most workers flunking. Apparently, according to Willard W. Wheeler's report of the same incident, Fee had not expected such a thorough-going racist reaction. Wheeler, one of the few staff members who supported Fee's stand on equality for Belle Mitchell, stated that Fee had cleared the matter with camp superintendent Colonel Jacques and with the man in charge of mess before bringing Belle Mitchell into the dining hall. Fee "supposed the coast was clear."[96]

Wheeler's contemporary account of the scene in the messroom is more detailed than Fee's *History* (written years afterward):

> The lady came and sat down at a small table where Bro. Fee sat. It was easy to see that her appearance created a sensation. The lady teachers soon began to absent themselves and Bro Williams seemed greatly ruffled. Col. Jacquess (who is also a Methodist minister) immediately fell to compromising as is their wont. He was afraid Bro. Fee had committed a great blunder, suggested that the young lady to be sent down to the "Soldier's Home" till the storm was overpast. Bro. F. refused. He [Jacques] said the Societies will not sustain you. Well then, I will stand alone. But Bro Fee I am Supt. of this home. Very well I will risk all on the issue. Then he [Jacques] flew right around and said I will have nothing to do with it. I will leave it with the mess. Thus washing his hands as Pilate did of old and with about as much effect in clearing his

skirts of his guilt. Henceforth Mr. Williams is the champion of the faction and the Col. went to Louisville on business. Now the disaffected in the mess prepare to besiege the camp of the uncircumcised. We daily went to our meals at the ringing of the bell, and they remained away till after we were through, meanwhile circulating a petition for the girl's removal from the house & table.

I give you a coppy [sic] of the communication addressed to Bro. F. by Bro. Williams. "Rev Mr Fee, your introduction into this house and to the table of a woman of color, without the consent of the occupants of it, and of those who conduct the mess, excites much comment and just repugnance to the act. There lies before me a written request signed by all the members of the mess with but two exceptions that I hereby signify to you the above fact and their united request that you withdraw from the table and the house at once the above mentioned person. A speedy compliance with the above will oblige.

I am yours etc.
L. Williams Jr.[97]

With heavy sarcasm, Wheeler analyzed Williams' communique and the entire situation: "You will notice," he wrote,

the crime which is charged upon your agent of 'introducing into the mess a *woman* of Color' and also the 'just repugnance' manifested at such atrocious conduct?

Fee, Wheeler reported, was "suffering very great persecution" at the hands of Williams and the other workers; their treatment of Fee was "cruel, vindictive & spiteful."[98]

Another of Fee's colleagues at the camp supported his action and reported on it to the American Missionary Association two days after the dining hall incident. Scofield, writing on September 1, 1865, was incredulous. "And will you believe it there was a general uproar among the teachers and superintendents because of it. The high bloods really refuse to eat in the same hall with her though they can sit at another table! And that too when they have employed half a dozen *black faces* to wait on them at the table and brush off the flies! *Shame!* [double underlining]"[99]

Fee's report at the time appears uncharacteristically reticent. Perhaps the business was too painful to explore fully. "We are having here," he wrote (September 1, 1865), "an hour of trial a rebellious spirit among some teachers from Cincinnati — over cast — & late hours. Also an order to break up the camp."[100]

About a week after the incident, another Camp Nelson worker reported. Mrs. Mary Colton, who had caused such a stir with her reaction to dancing, addressed herself to the Belle Mitchell story. (The order to throw Mrs. Colton out of camp had not been carried out.) In spite of her inhibitive morality in matters of little consequence, Mrs. Colton revealed a surprising spirit of tolerance. First, she described Belle Mitchell: her father was a white man, her mother a quadroon. The parents were married, living together in Danville, members of the Methodist church there; Belle was also a member of that church. Second, Mrs. Colton gave her version of Fee's motivation as she understood it: "Knowing the wants of the school & believing it would have a favorable impression on the colored people here & also was her right, & should be her privilege to teach her own color, Bro. Fee proposed to her to come. He had heard her highly spoken of...."[101]

Like Wheeler's version, Mrs. Colton's account rings with indignant sarcasm:

> But lo! what an insult to the good abolition missionary teachers from Mass. & Ohio. [Mrs. Colton, like Fee was from Bracken County, Kentucky] They refused to come to their tables to eat while we were at our meals.

She went on to describe an altercation between Mrs. Williams and herself, an occasion when the two ladies almost came to blows.[102]

On September 14, 1865, Fee returned to Camp Nelson from Berea, where two of his children had been sick and where he had performed the marriage of his daughter Laura. He found on his arrival that Colonel Jacques had sent Belle Mitchell *and* Mrs. Colton and her daughter Anna Smith out of the camp. In addition, by Jacques' order, Fee was no longer superintendent — his post had been given to Ann Williams. Fee's report to the American Missionary Association is one of the saddest he ever filed:

> Miss Mitchell as I have told you is *slightly* colored — features not African (I speak as a fool) She was very exemplary in conduct.
>
> When advised by Mrs. Colton 'to stay until Bro Fee should come' Miss Mitchell replied, "I must go. Col. Jacques told me I must to day (Saturday) or tomorrow." She told him she could not Saturday — clothing out to wash — & that Sabbath she did not wish to use as a day of traveling!
>
> On Monday Bell went home — This was not because her help was not needed as a teacher.

On the contrary, he said, the need was "great."

Miss Mitchell at time said to Mrs. Williams there are scores of children yet in camp who could be gathered into school if we had teachers.

During my absence Mrs. Williams returned here and Col Jacques placed her as superintendent of the schools and this morning I have a note from his clerk saying Mrs. Williams is placed as superintendent of the schools and you are therefore relieved from all further duty as superintendent of the schools. By order of Col. Jas. F. Jacques.

When Fee arrived in Camp, Jacques was gone, having left Williams in charge. "And this," Fee protested,

after telling me he believed the interests here required the removal of all & the putting in of other officers. Pilate & Herod made friends over the slain body of Jesus — Miss Mitchell.

I cannot endorse such a school — its moral effect is now only a curse — a baptism of the spirit of cast — the lesson daily taught to each child — "After all you are only niggers."[103]

At this point, understandably, Fee felt the place for him was Berea. He had the confidence of the black people both at Camp Nelson and in Madison County — "5,000 there," he said. Leaving Camp Nelson would not involve abandoning his work with ex-slaves.

On September 15, 1865, Fee wrote to the American Missionary Association asking for money to pay Belle Mitchell for her short stint of teaching. He also reported that Willard W. Wheeler had moved from supervising in Camp Nelson to teaching at Berea. Mrs. Wheeler, Fee believed, would also be an asset at Berea; she was in excellent health, he reported, and would be confined in December. "Bro. Wheeler," Fee wrote, "I regard as a true good man." Fee's confidence in Wheeler and his friendship for him had been won by Wheeler's clear and decisive...words and actions for impartial treatment to all worthy people," his words and actions in the Belle Mitchell case.[104]

Fee found it difficult to get away from the camp, where the school was definitely running down. Colonel Jacques opposed his leaving, although why Fee should have retained any respect for Jacques' orders is unclear.[105]

Fee had written to the American Missionary Association, asking for their judgment on the caste question. Their answer was slow in coming, perhaps slow in being formulated. Meantime, he wrote them again (September 20, 1865) making it clear that his position would not change, no matter what they decided at their New York headquarters. Staying at the camp, he expected antagonism from Jacques, the Williamses and anyone they would hire. With his son Burritt, the Wheelers, Scofield, Mrs. Smith and her daughter gone from the camp, Fee was alone and prepared to stand alone, even if the whole American Missionary Association opposed his position. "The world needs to be converted," he wrote, "not to Methodism or Presbyterianism or Baptism, but to principle — to *Christ* the personification of all principle; and the man or society that eliminates — hold up the right principle — a correct standard by which the world shall be converted does an *infinite good to the world*. Here is a case clear and favorable. You will not let it slip through your fingers I feel shure [sic]."[106]

The case continued to draw accounts from others of the camp staff. Mrs. Caroline Daimon, employed by the American Missionary Association, wrote on September 23 to defend herself. She began by referring to the dancing incident, denying that she had ever danced or ever seen anyone dancing. Nothing happened, she said. "One evening a gentleman who is an amateur performer upon the violin was playing a waltz and one of the young ladies in the most innocent manner skipped upon the Hall floor with one of the boarders. Some minds 'strain at a gnat and swallow a camel.'" However, Mrs. Daimon admitted, she had signed the petition against Belle Mitchell.[107]

On September 26, Fee wrote to report an ugly sequence of events. Jacques had hurriedly left Camp Nelson at the point of crisis, because he had business in Louisville. "Last evening," Fee wrote, "Louisville Press brought the published account of the arrest of our superintendent Colonel Jacquess for complicity in a case of abortion & consequent death in 8 hours of his paramour or 'mistress' a 'Georgia woman.' He left here on pretence of going to his family in Illinois, went to Louisville wrote back he was sick there. He was arrested by the police in the work of procuring abortion." Jacques was a Methodist minister, Fee pointed out, who had preached at the camp himself.[108]

Mrs. Williams had told Fee "with much feeling (and repeatedly).... You brought the young lady [Miss Mitchell] into this trouble." On September 27, Lester Williams reported to the American Missionary Association that Fee was a "liar" and "a falsifier," "treacherous and hypocritical." Mrs. Williams wrote the next day to say that she defied anyone to prove that she had treated Belle Mitchell "otherwise than with entire respect." "My whole bearing toward her, & conversation with her," she wrote, "was such as I would give a sister or ask *for* a sister. Furthermore, I will add that I am probably as rabid and consistent an abolitionist as yourself."[109]

On September 30, Fee reported that General Fisk was eager to break up the camp within 17 days. But a new episode had taken place in the Belle Mitchell case: "Miss Belle Mitchell came here yesterday," Fee stated. "She went to the dinner table with Anna Smith, daughter of Mrs. Colton. Genl. Barrett, the new superintendent, called for her, Anna Smith & myself after dinner — said to Miss Mitchell 'You cannot come to the table when I am here.' Other things were said. I think we have evidence that our schools, as suggested before, must be free from government officials." Although Fee was still considering schools at both Camp Nelson and Berea, this latter statement points to one more advantage of the Berea location. (By September, 1865, Willard W. Wheeler was conducting school at Berea with 10 students.)[110]

Meanwhile the American Missionary Association had taken decisive action in the Belle Mitchell affair. On September 28, a committee was sent to Camp Nelson from Cincinnati (Levi Coffin among them) and required all American Missionary Association "teachers to sign a paper declaring they would not make complexion a condition of association among teachers." Evidently these signatures were difficult to obtain, as Fee wrote, "This was wormed out after a long time of working."[111]

One teacher, Joseph C. Chapin, wrote to the American Missionary Association on October 2, claiming he only signed the petition vs. Belle Mitchell because he saw her presence caused unpleasant feelings, and he wanted to restore peace. "Her Color ," he wrote, "was no objection to any one so far as I can learn. Her conduct (which was exemplary as far as I know) was no objection, simply the manner in which she was thrust into the family, that and that alone, was the objection with all, I believe, except myself." This bit of white-washing reveals how eager the former Camp Nelson abolitionists were to conceal their own prejudice from themselves and one another.[112]

On October 2, 1865, Fee filed a summary report of his time at Camp Nelson, enumerating all that had been accomplished and lamenting all that might disappear at the dissolution of the camp. "Fifteen months since I came to this camp — I came to encourage & help the soldiers, especially the colored men of our state who were then enlisting and needed an instructor and a comforter."[113]

At Hall's suggestion, Fee had organized schools for non-commissioned officers in colored regiments. Soon he had a large school, with 13 teachers at one period, and soon the schools extended to privates and children. Hundreds of soldiers had been instructed. "A considerable number learned not only to read, but also to write, and now, from the army in Texas send letters to their families and friends in the camp."

A church had been organized, the "church of Christ at Camp Nelson, Ky.," which now had 81 members, but thousands had attended it. A refugee home had been prepared. "Here were erected four large wards, dining hall, school building, containing seven rooms, ninety seven cottages, two rooms in each, sixty government tents and fifty cabins erected by the colored people." At one time, the camp contained as many as 3,060 women and children. A school had been organized within the Refugee Home, where more than 600 children had been regularly taught.

"I do not believe any class of children learn faster than these," Fee wrote, "Few schools of white children [are] so good in behavior."[114]

After all this, the camp was to be broken up by order of the War Department.

On October 4, 1865, a Reverend Edward P. Smith wrote to the American Missionary Association to suggest a black school in Lexington where Belle Mitchell might work as a teacher. A few days later Mary Colton reported that Belle would take charge of the school, a free school for children of black soldiers.[115]

Ann Williams, unrepentent, resigned her Camp Nelson post on October 11, 1865. Her husband, however, persisted in writing letters of self-defense. He maintained that his action had been against Fee, not against Belle Mitchell. "If your neighbor should introduce a black man into your house & invite him to sit down at your table, you would be very apt to think you should have something to say about it." Having sealed the case against himself, Williams at last withdrew from the scene.[116]

On the same day (October 18) Scofield wrote: "We are every day hoping to be relieved of the presence of Mr. & Mrs. Williams and think there will be a little more both peace and freedom when they are gone. The hypocrisy and falsehood they have practiced toward brother Fee and Bell Mitchell ought to be exposed. The malice to all of which seems to have been malice toward J. G. Fee." In the same vein, Scofield added, "I am doing something in looking after the affairs of the [black] soldiers. Many of them suffer great wrong from their white oppressors, officers and citizens together conspire to cheat and plunder them."[117]

Ironically, as the citizens of Camp Nelson looked forward to peace and freedom, the camp rapidly broke up. Mrs. Daimon reported the schools closed at Camp Nelson on October 20, 1865. Fee advised the American Missionary Association to act rapidly and procure the government buildings at Camp Nelson for continued use as a school.[118]

Wheeler reported that he was prospering in the Berea School (October 30, 1865), even though Fee was not there. On November 1, Fee visited the colored schools in Lexington and saw Belle Mitchell, who had assumed her teaching position. He recommended her for an American Missionary Association commission and observed, "There are some excellent colored men in Lexington." Rogers was bent on going to Berea, Scofield had decided to stay at Camp Nelson and Fee seriously considered going to Lexington, where he saw another open door, where black people wanted him.[119]

In part, Fee's decision to return to Berea was simply personal: his son Burritt was very sick in November, 1865, and Fee wanted to nurse the young man himself. In addition, Fee had organized a colored school in Berea, which Ellen Wheeler had conducted with some success. It increased constantly, and by November 30, 1865, she had 20 pupils. (Mrs. Wheeler was the first person to teach black people officially in Berea — a distinction to be noted.) The "colored men [at Camp Nelson]," Fee wrote, "are very anxious to get homes there [Berea] in order to educate their children." Five black families had applied to him in November, and he felt a farm of 119 acres, which the Bereans had recently purchased, might be parcelled out to black settlers. Rogers and Hanson, both at Berea by this time, desired Fee's help in getting the school on foot. All these considerations led to Fee's final decision. But the most important single factor seems to have been his plan to procure land for blacks.[120]

"There is a consideration of importance to us all," he wrote,

> that is a *homestead* for the colored man. In the "Blue Grass" — fertile portion of Central Ky., men own large farms & to grass, cattle & mules. At present they are not disposed to sell to "niggers." The colored man there must be a hireling, an attachee — Many very many are buying small lots about the towns & putting small houses upon them & then depend upon "day's work" — here some will fall into want & steal then a "hugh [sic] & cry" will be against them. They need to be encouraged to go out into the hill country — even to the mountain counties & there spend their four or five hundred dollars (as these soldiers have) in getting a home that will *support them*.
>
> Let enough get into a neighborhood to sustain a school & church there — not all into one county — scatter into different counties — and *as at Berea intersperse with some white friends*. [Italics my own]
>
> By my position out at the foot of the mountain region I may attract — I can attract many — if I only had a company at my hand who would buy out several farmers & then *parcel* to colored men as well as whites. Then I would take to them the teachers & missionary through you.[121]

In and around the town of Berea, interspersion of the races became a reality.[122]

In November, 1865, Belle Mitchell filed a report as a new worker for the American Missionary Association. Several students in her school were sick, others did not have sufficient clothing. "The children seem to learn with a willing mind," she wrote. Fee, having visited her school, affirmed that she was doing well and was willing to go on

Burritt Fee — John G. Fee's eldest son and his helper in Camp Nelson work.

Courtesy of Berea College Archives

teaching for $15 a month. He had preached again to the black people in Lexington. "There are many there who are bright men & women and the children very hopeful," he wrote. "They express quite a desire to have me come & help manage their schools — also preach to them. You would be much gratified to witness the change of public sentiment there. Many white men of intelligence & position talked with me freely & sympathizingly on the subject of the education of these colored people — feel that they are here and *will stay* and that it is best for all to have them educated." The son of Judge William C. Goodloe, prominent in Kentucky politics, wanted to head an agency for educating colored men.[123]

"If Berea is to be started anew," Fee said, "now is the time." John Rogers arrived in Berea on December 1, 1865, prepared to become principal of the new school which would become Berea College. On December 8, Fee reported that Mrs. Wheeler had been teaching her colored school for two months (at a rate of $21 per month). During December, Camp Nelson had only two teachers left, Mrs. Colton and her daughter, but Willard Wheeler reported 60 students at Berea, where his school had been sustained entirely by the District. Berea was growing again, while Camp Nelson was disintegrating.[124]

In fact, Berea was growing at Camp Nelson's expense. On December 16, 1865 Fee wrote, "Families are scattering from here [Camp Nelson] and settling around Berea." Still he was at Camp Nelson when the facilities went up for sale, trying to get buildings for a possible school.[125]

Gabriel Burdett, still in the Union army, had been detailed by General Fisk, at Fee's request, to help find homes for refugees leaving Camp Nelson. Burdett had toured Madison County by this time. Fee urged the American Missionary Association to pay him. Burdett had to hire a horse for his journeys and he had a wife and two children, besides a sister-in-law with nine children, dependent on his support. Pay him, Fee said, "I know he needs it." Besides, Fee added, "I think him *eminently* useful."[126]

In general, Fee feared that the graft and hypocrisy of white people would make it impossible for blacks to trust "any white face." He suggested that the American Missionary Association hire an agent to make business deals for black people seeking homes. "May I employ some honest man," he asked, "to meet the wants of these people as they shall wish to settle near Berea?"[127]

By January 6, 1866, Fee himself was settled permanently in Berea for the first time in years. He reported,

> Our school is now under care of our board of trustees and is starting with good prospects. We propose to build a new school room & in the primary department put in colored & white children. We wish to employ such a teacher as we *know* one who shall be so well qualified & so excellent in person, manner &c as to override prejudice & bigotry and command respect to the school for her sake & for Christ's sake.[128]

6. The Legacy of Camp Nelson

Berea became Fee's primary work from 1866 on, but his connection with Camp Nelson did not end when he returned to Berea. He maintained his interest in the projects there until his death, serving as a trustee for the Camp Nelson school, Ariel Academy, for years. (He left several small bequests to the Camp Nelson school in his will, along with similar bequests to Berea College.) In addition, two workers from Camp Nelson, Willard and Ellen Wheeler, became part of Berea College's first teaching staff, and two others, Abisha Scofield and Gabriel Burdett, served on the board of trustees of Berea while still working at Camp Nelson. With the election of Gabriel Burdett April 12, 1866, the board of trustees of Berea College was established on an interracial basis. He served as the first (and at that time the only) black trustee from 1866-1878.[129]

From Camp Nelson, Berea received a legacy of tangible and intangible benefits. First and foremost, Berea College gained most of its early black students directly from Camp Nelson. Some had been soldiers there, others were children of soldiers. Many families who had been refugees in Camp Nelson settled around Berea. The black settlers, while many had been members of slave families native to Madison

County, had frequently spent part of the war years in Camp Nelson. The Ballards, for example, an important black family in the Reconstruction years at Berea (and later — descendants of this family are still connected with Berea College), had been Madison County slaves for generations but moved to the area around Berea from Camp Nelson. Many black students at Berea before 1904 bore the names of Madison County white families. It seems likely that the Ballards traced a common pattern: from some portion of Madison County, usually the Bluegrass region, to Camp Nelson, then back to Madison County as settlers in or near Berea.[130]

Virtually all the first black students at Berea had been born into slavery; many had also been refugees; some were probably part of the group expelled from Camp Nelson in November, 1864. They had suffered incredible hardships, and at John G. Fee's invitation they came to Berea as a haven — at Berea they could buy land of their own, attend a college where they would be welcome, live on the basis of equality with sympathetic white citizens.

Of the intangible benefits Berea received from Camp Nelson, the most obvious is simply described: at Camp Nelson, Fee and the soldiers and refugees had struck up a love relationship that was to extend throughout his life. His "face and character" had become "known to thousands." Berea would never lack black students as long as Fee was physically able to reach them. Listening to Fee became a tradition among the blacks of Kentucky. They regarded him with respect and genuine affection; they called him "Father" Fee, and they followed him to Berea by the hundreds. They trusted him as they trusted no other white man in the state.[131]

At Camp Nelson, Fee had passed all the tests that many of his fellow abolitionists failed. After slavery was abolished, it became all too clear that many had called for the end of slavery who could not welcome freed men and women as their equals. Fee, at Camp Nelson, certified his own beliefs in undeniable action. The black people of Kentucky rightly trusted him, since he had demonstrated his own trustworthiness repeatedly and unmistakably.

Camp Nelson provided bitter lessons for Fee, which shaped his attitude toward teachers and students at Berea as long as he lived. Mere administration struck him as meaningless; kindness was better than administration. He had learned that some colleagues could voice concern for black persons without having any real love for them. He had seen how power and authority appealed to those white people who chose a life of "service" to blacks.

But most importantly (and positively), Fee had tested his own ideas concerning equality — genuinely equal treatment brought forth from former slaves the most miraculous results: eagerness to learn, hard work and dedication. In many respects Fee, from his Christian perspective, saw that black people were better than whites, more trusting, more open, with genuine humility and piety. In every respect, he perceived, they were potentially equal — these present black people, not some future generation: those who could not read could rapidly learn; those who could not care for their own business transactions could learn. All their apparent deficiencies in the white world could be eliminated. Unlike many white educators of this period (and later) Fee showed no inclination to turn black people into white people as quickly as possible. He wanted education for them but not transformation into dark-skinned Anglo-Saxon Protestants. In fact, Camp Nelson had left John G. Fee more than a little disillusioned with white Christians, whose piety too frequently formed only a thin overlay for poisonous racism. After all, Fee received more favorable reactions from his black friends than from anyone else. Why change those who approved of him and loved him into those who mostly despised and spurned him? For blacks, Fee remained a hero; by whites increasingly he was called a fanatic. For the former, the image of Fee was as their champion and defender, ministering to the sick and dying, teaching and preaching, defying all the powers that be to maintain black freedom and equality. For the latter, his image was to become that of a man who rose to condemn a young lady skipping down the hall with an undertaker while the fiddler played a waltz.

II. THE SOLUTION OF BEREA

1. Berea's Black Settlers

One aspect of Berea's early history has never received particular attention: the black settlers of the region and the town, the black founding families. They came in great numbers, for safety, for company, for love of John G. Fee, for education for their children. For almost 40 years — the term of Berea's first interracial experiment — for almost two human generations, the black families of Berea supported the project. That Berea was *forced* to fail in its goals for interracial education should not obscure what was actually achieved from 1866-1904. And the black people who lived and worked in Berea from the beginning should not be forgotten.

Many individuals and families came from Camp Nelson. It is impossible now to determine how many. Fee's testimony shows that he invited black families and individual black soldiers to the Berea settlement. He indicates that many accepted his invitation. Available evidence bears out Fee's remarks. The Ballards and Walkers, for example, originally Madison County slave families, were taken to Camp Nelson and returned to settle near Berea, where dozens of members of both families attended the school. Sampson [Simpson] Gentry (father of many Berea black students), a native of Madison County, born a slave near Richmond, served in the Union Army and was hospitalized for eight weeks at Camp Nelson. When his army service ended, he moved to Big Hill, and then in 1872 to Berea. Like Gentry, Berea settlers Alexander Miller and Anderson White were members of Company K, 13th U.S. Colored Artillery (Heavy), and were stationed at Camp Nelson. Many fathers of black families settling in Berea had been soldiers: Horace Yates, Gordon Glascoe, Henry Adams, Alexander Chenault, Larkin Farris, John Moss, Stephen Willis, and others; virtually all may be assumed to have become connected with Berea by meeting Fee at Camp Nelson.[132]

2. Fee's Theories of Racial Relations

Fee's ideas about racial relations and his policies for interracial education were formed in a crucible of action at Camp Nelson and Berea. For years, his thinking seems to have been shaped by actual events in his life, so that his plans, especially for Berea College, remained intensely practical, rooted in action, never merely theoretical.

In November, 1866, Reverend Abisha Scofield was driven out of Camp Nelson. The incident was fraught with violence. A mob dragged him and his son from his room and made them promise to leave. One black man, John Burnsides, "fought like a tiger & killed an attacker," but was soon overpowered himself, "knocked down & left for dead." The mob fired shots through his house at the women and children, then pursued Scofield's daughter, but she hid and they missed her. They then set fire to the houses, but the fire went out.[133]

Scofield, at Camp Nelson, had — as Fee said — no social protection: "Not one white family." This situation left him totally vulnerable, but blacks at Camp Nelson were exposed as well, with no whites among them. Fee saw that, practically speaking, progress toward racial equality in society, required numbers of both white and black people working together for mutual protection. An advantage to inviting former soldiers to settle in Berea is obvious — if the enemies of Berea chose to attack, trained fighters might give the most effective response.[134]

Another problem at Camp Nelson, less dramatic than mob violence, but perhaps more serious in the long run, was the refusal of the man who owned all the available land at the camp to sell it to black people. This was, of course, only a particular instance of a wholesale problem. The reluctance of whites, all over the South, to see black people become property owners was often part of a movement to reduce former slaves to peonage. People without property of their own must become dependent on those who controlled the economy. In regions where blacks were effectively blocked from land ownership, they were quickly restored to a state closely resembling slavery, frequently by former masters. When economic and social pressures were brought to bear, blacks were forced to retain habits of servility, forced, indeed, to act like slaves, even though their freedom had been granted.[135]

These practical concerns and others helped John G. Fee formulate the working hypotheses of Berea's new community and college. "Young colored men," he wrote, "out of sight of their former masters & with those who treat them as brethren lose their *servile habits,* acquire self respect and independent, self-reliant habits." While Fee saw the necessity for introducing blacks to a new form of social intercourse with whites, he also emphasized the need of white people to learn new ways. "So with young white men in a society where the controlling influence is to treat the colored man as a moral legal social equal he forms the habit of doing so much more readily than he would where there is a proud rich aristocracy overawing."[136]

"We need a place," he said,

> where the school, church & society are on a right basis or principle of action — there let the youth be until they shall form the *habit* of right action. This is part of the requisite education. We do not propose that they go into a cloister — no, but that we shall form a *society,* somewhere, radically different from the proud cast feeling, sectarian society so general in the south.

"Somewhere" would be Berea.

Fee did not want a mere black school which would be just as good as a mere white school, "but would not be a true sentiment of the gospel, & a high interest of society & *national well being,* be promoted by the mutual recognition & free social communion of both classes. This is honestly, & kindly & widely done here [in Berea] — with much harmony."

The society Fee envisioned, which he and others attempted to embody at Berea, required both whites and blacks in equal numbers. Because of Berea's unique position, Fee saw it as clearly ideal for his purposes: "We are in the 'hill country,'" he wrote, "Between the 'blue grass' & the mountains. From the former region we now draw our colored men, from the latter the young white men & ladies. We should not be far removed from the latter. They are a desirable element." The other school locations Fee considered (Camp Nelson and Lexington) had the distinct disadvantage that no white people could be induced to go to them. Berea, on the other hand, had "a historic association...of no small value at home & abroad." For himself Fee said, "The crowning consideration [was] a *practical recognition of the brotherhood of man.*"[137]

His idea of "practical recognition" emerged clearly in a letter (written January 25, 1867) in which he dealt with the question of how to use one of Berea's first large donations of money, the Avery Fund, designated "for education & *elevation* of the *colored* race." "I believe," Fee wrote,

> there is no way in which we can so successfully *elevate* the colored race as in schools where their true manhood shall be honestly practically & freely recognized.
>
> Not to flatter them — elate them — but accustom them to a practical moral & social equality, in the school, in the Lyceum, in the church, in all — (along with white pupils)

is...an important part of his education. We are likely here to have so many white pupils male & females that we can give to the colored youth this *practical* recognition.

Also here the number of white pupils will not likely be so overwhelming that the colored pupil will feel that any courtesy to him is a mere matter of condescencion to him as a feeble minority.

Fee stated that he was "reconciled" to Berea. He thought it "a good place for the education & elevation of the colored race," because he believed that "colored men must gravitate to the mountains for *homes*" and because he perceived "the moral power [in Berea] of an impartial & practical recognition of the manhood of the black man."[138]

Fee wanted to expend money directly on black young men and women, keeping them constantly in school until they were fitted for the position of teachers. Desiring to keep tuition and board low as an inducement, Fee suggested using endowment income in direct aid to blacks. As a matter of fact, Berea's black students were encouraged to teach while they attended school. So some blacks from Berea, along with a few black students from Oberlin, taught in Freedmen's Schools in Kentucky during this early period (1866-70). Angus Burleigh, for example, conducted a school in Garrard County in 1869. John H. Jackson instructed a class in Madison County in 1868. And Cornelius C. Vaughan taught a day school and a night school for his people in Cynthiana in 1869 and in Richmond in 1870.[139]

3. Fee's Policies: Interracial Education in a Community Context and Interspersion

Fee's scheme for interracial education required, from the beginning, a total social context. The relationship of school to church and community was integral to his conception of practical recognition of equality. It was never enough, on his view, to teach equality without having the means to practice it, and he would have considered it pointless to speak of a person possessing a right, if that right could not be enjoyed. Even though his plans began at a very specific, local level, he envisioned a school which would contribute to "national well being" by its active demonstration of principles. Berea was intended as a sign for the entire United States.

Part of the reason for Berea's early success — and those 40 years of actual interracial education *must* be construed as a success — sprang directly from one of Fee's most daring and effective ideas. He had determined that Berea would be the place where black people could own property of their own. He did not wish to promote a system of *apartheid* ownership, however, but insisted on a kind of "interspersion": all black people should not live apart, but blacks and whites should be interspersed about the countryside and in the town. In the 1860's and '70's, Fee's "interspersion" policy became successful in action.[140]

It worked very well. Fee himself, many of the resident trustees, and a small group of Berea supporters provided black settlers with land of their own, on terms they could afford, with practical help at every stage. Blacks were unfamiliar with business practices — what experience had they had, after all, in buying land? The Bereans not only sold to blacks but helped them conduct their affairs until they could stand on their own.

Some 40 families of blacks (probably more) should be considered founding families of Berea. These people arrived in the area between 1866 and 1870. Most obtained homes and land of their own, through Fee's influence. In some cases the family would locate near Berea and buy land some years later (in the 1870's and '80's), but virtually all acquired property eventually. Some lived within the village of Berea itself, and many others bought farms nearby, on Brushy Fork especially, and northeast of Berea where Middletown is now located.

One family of white Bereans sold hundreds of acres to black settlers: Joel Todd, Sr., and his wife Nancy, exiled from Berea for their abolitionist sympathies in 1860, made land available to many black families. Other Berea families, all early supporters of Fee's abolitionist ministry, most also exiles, sold lesser quantities of land to former slaves.[141]

In addition, of course, Fee himself, Hanson, Rogers and other Berea staff members sold houses and land to blacks routinely. In 1876, a detailed land-ownership map of Madison County, Kentucky, was published. It printed the name of every land-owner in the county and pinpointed the location of his/her holdings. The region around Berea was divided almost equally between whites and blacks. While the black families were concentrated in a couple of places — near Brushy Fork and in present Middletown — they were also widely dispersed, and virtually no black family owned land without a boundary on some white person's property. The reverse was also true: virtually all white people around Berea had black neighbors.[142]

To appreciate Fee's enormous influence in this matter of land sales, we must realize that (with very few exceptions) *only* the supporters of Berea (those who had been exiles or the trustees) conducted land transactions with black people in the region. This seems to have remained true for almost 50 years.

A later printed map, undated, probably from the late 1880's or early '90's, shows town lots of Berea and designates, in pencilled notations, owners of all land. Once again, blacks are definitely not living all in the same corner of town; black owners are identified up and down the main street. The effect is not quite a checkerboard, but it does not even approach a ghetto pattern. Fee's interspersion theory was developed and applied: probably no other community in the South resembled Berea in its pattern of interspersed land ownership.[143]

Some of Berea's black citizens, former slaves who arrived in town virtually destitute, became prosperous enough to write wills. Ned Blythe, for example, made specific bequests to his many children, as did Anderson Crawford and others: they rose from slaves to men of property in a few years. Fee intended to help every black person to the same basic opportunities: he believed a complete education required a total social and religious commitment.[144]

4. The New School: 1866

Berea Literary Institute, supervised by the College board of trustees, reopened in January, 1866, with John A. R. Rogers as principal, and Willard W. Wheeler and Eliza Snedaker as assistant teachers. During the opening term the school was housed in the district building. The trustees of the district school had asked Fee to secure a teacher, and in exchange they would give the use of the district house to the Berea College trustees "to do what they [pleased] with it." As the only trustee on the ground, Fee took all necessary actions. He procured the services of Wheeler, his fellow worker from Camp Nelson, as district teacher for the term, with the understanding that the next session of the school would have provisions for "impartial education" — black students as well as white.[145]

Wheeler agreed to Fee's proposal, and his wife Ellen P. T. Wheeler also assented. Along with his district school teaching, Wheeler undertook to tutor black students in preparation for their entrance to Berea, while Mrs. Wheeler taught a small class of primary students in her home, only eight or nine children, but all black — perhaps the first organized teaching of Negroes in Madison County. Thus, before Berea College reopened, its purpose was clear — the school was to be integrated. The idea for such a school had been formed years earlier, but in 1865, Fee's first positive action as a trustee was to insure that the college he was founding should be anti-caste. Fee was the only trustee directly involved in this momentous step.[146]

Other educators in the South of this period — Lyman Abbott, for example — considered attempting to bring blacks and poor whites into schools together. When Abbott asked Clinton Fisk, Freedmen's Bureau Commissioner for Kentucky and Tennessee, about the possibility, Fisk replied "that it could not be done," because both classes opposed it. Separate schools under the same organization might, but "he knew of no successful experiment in mixing the races." "In practice, white children, with few exceptions, refused to attend institutions run by Northern societies. They were determined not to associate with blacks in this way, they disliked the idea of charity schools and they hated "Yankee Schoolmarms." Fisk's pronouncements on the impossibility of an interracial school were issued in April, 1866, only a month after Berea's educational experiment began to contradict this conventional wisdom.[147]

5. Fee's Political Labors for Black Equality

Fee's other activities during this crucial period of Berea's history reveal how the new interracial school matched his total vision of equality for blacks. Education had become central to Fee's program — in addition to the school he had organized at Camp Nelson, Fee had set up schools among blacks in adjacent counties and tried "to establish county aid societies among benevolent whites...to assist the [black] schools." He encouraged blacks to set up schools and churches of their own "to prepare themselves for freedom."[148]

When blacks of Camp Nelson assembled to celebrate the Fourth of July in 1865, Fee spoke to them enthusiastically in favor of Negro suffrage. Later that year, he addressed blacks in Louisville, Lexington, Danville and Camp Nelson and "frankly encouraged [them] to anticipate the day when the vote would be theirs." After the Kentucky legislature denied blacks equal rights in the courts, Fee attended a statewide convention of blacks in Lexington on March 26, 1866. A "Declaration of Sentiments" and resolutions were adopted which "expressed faith that the legislature would 'ere long' grant them their 'just and natural rights.'" The convention affirmed that Negroes were entitled to "each and every right and power guaranteed to every American citizen."[149]

On July 4, 1867, Fee spoke at the "Colored People's Barbecue" in Lexington, advocating impartial suffrage before a massive audience of 6,000-10,000 blacks. "God was the author of the Emancipation Proclamation, the Civil Rights Bill," Fee said, "and would soon give suffrage to the freedmen." At the same meeting, the civil rights question was discussed, with Fee supporting the position that black testimony must be admitted in court.[150]

Another Negro State Convention, in Lexington on November 26, 1867, had Fee on the platform again speaking in favor of black suffrage. The president of this meeting, R. T. James, a clergyman from Louisville, said, "We claim the right to vote in the name of Liberty that has been purchased by colored soldiers," a position Fee supported.[151]

In the first years of Berea's post-war existence, John G. Fee established himself as a major spokesmen for black liberation in Kentucky. His presence at the most important political meetings of black citizens in Kentucky bespeaks his high position in their esteem. Clearly, Berea College was only one part of Fee's program for the benefit of the freed slaves of his native state, although Berea was to be a summation of Fee's work, growing out of his educational and religious goals, an attempt to embody his ideals of justice and equality.

In January, 1866, Fee wrote to the American Missionary Association describing the new school and analyzing its prospects:

> We are now getting up another charter [for Berea] preparing to go before the benevolent public, soon, for aid. The trustees of the District School however are not ready for us to put colored children in with the white yet — say we may after this term is out — first of March. We have now about sixty white pupils in the school and almost 20 colored ready to go in soon as we shall have a new building ready for all.
>
> Bro. Rogers is in the school part of his time. He hears two or three classes each day & gives one scientific lecture each week — & one bible lecture 30 minutes....
>
> The school either at Camp Nelson or at Lexington will be essentially a colored school — perhaps wholy [sic] so. Here it will be mixed — probably the colored are coming fastest and many more will come if we give them a 'fair show.' This may result in the running away of the 'whitefolks.' We think we will make the school so excellent that the whitefolks will stay for the sake of the advantages and after a time outgrow former prejudices.
>
> I have made efforts to get colored ministers here as you suggested to Bro. Rogers. They do not come as yet. The colored people are not migratory — their knowledge is limited; they have strong home associations.
>
> We could have more pupils of each class by having our schools separate — schools for whites & schools for blacks; and perhaps prejudice will not be overcome until the colored people shall have education, culture, and acquire property & habits of cleanliness.
>
> But in view of the hostile feeling likely to exist between the two races because of ill treatment of the colored people, will not our school at Berea have a good significance and effect even if not large?[152]

Many years later, Fee described the original design of the founders and early patrons of Berea: to build "a school where the colored man could have equal facilities with white men, and where the colored man would have such a measure of social and Christian kindness as would inspire in him that measure of self-respect as would make him easy and comfortable in all meritorious circles."[153]

Throughout the controversies and hardships that lay ahead, Fee remained faithful to his vision of Berea College as a sign, a light on a hill — the mission of Berea was to foster interracial equality, to serve as an example for the entire nation, a goal from which he never deviated.

6. First Term (January 2-March 29, 1866): Integration of the School

In the spring of 1866, Berea College (or "Literary Institution," as it was then known) produced a promotional leaflet asking for donations. The school was "open to *all* of good moral character": thus Berea's proclamation appeared before the "benevolent" world — the new school would be for black as well as white, for female as well as male, for the poor instead of the rich. The principles of Berea, by the time this advertisement appeared, had been dramatically expressed in action.

On March 6, 1866 — a red-letter day in Berea's history — the school became interracial in practice. Rogers wrote in his *Journal:* "Four colored children entered the school. Eighteen of the students left. There was no little excitement. Twenty five remained. The Lord was with us to bless and cheer." Fee's report of the incident to the American Missionary Association: "Yesterday the colored children entered our school here — quite a number of white children left, more than half — those who remain in the Academic Department are all professed Christians — about 12 or 15 — they are very hopeful — my two sons are among them. This is our time of trial." Another contemporary writer, Willard W. Wheeler reported on the incident to the board of trustees (March 31, 1866) and later described (November 22, 1866) consequences of the events in March. In his report he stated that 27 members of the school had "unceremoniously and in a very disrespectful manner left the school." But their absence had been compensated by the addition of 18 black students within the month. According to his November summary, after the walkout, the District Trustees refused the use of their house to the Bereans, even though they had known beforehand about the admission of black children. About two-thirds of the white students left, Wheeler said, and "most [people] prophesied another mob and the total annihilation of the school." The faculty and students went on and mounted an exhibition at the end of term.[154]

During the first term of the new school, John G. Fee, his attention focused primarily on Berea again, increased his work and his responsibilities with a broad range of concerns in addition to his political activities. At the end of January, he and Rogers met all black ministers of Madison County to seek recruits for Berea. By February 3, Fee had "increased [his] family with two colored persons," one of whom was Angus Burleigh (mentioned below). Fee's relationships with blacks included familial intimacy from this period on.[155]

Fee had, he reported, aided Belle Mitchell in her new Lexington school for black children, by teaching himself from November 20-December 20, 1865. He sought, it would seem, virtually every form of involvement with black people he could sustain: his was not a distant patronage of a "lowly" race but a continual interaction with other human beings, an interaction he continued for the rest of his life. Fee, probably one of the stubbornest men who ever lived, was, by the same token, one of the most faithful.[157]

7. Second Term (April 16-June, 1866): Angus Burleigh, Soldier-Student from Camp Nelson

In terms of financial support, Berea's second term as an integrated school was altogether hopeful, but the teaching staff still consisted only of Rogers, Wheeler and Snedaker. Several black children were added to the ranks of the students early in the second term, which began with a total enrollment of 70. White students and the surrounding community had evidently accepted the presence of black children in the Primary Department.[157]

When black soldiers began to arrive, controversy was renewed. In late April or early May, 1866, Angus Augustus Burleigh, age 18, a mulatto, entered the school. He had been a sergeant in Company G, 12th U.S. Colored Artillery (Heavy), mustered in at Camp Nelson August 22, 1864. Fee had found him there and invited him to become a student at Berea. When he arrived, Burleigh was the first black adult to enroll in the institution (he was to become one of the first black men graduated from Berea College — class of 1875 — and he lived to be [in 1934] Berea's oldest living graduate).[158]

Son of an Englishman and a slave, Burleigh was born on a ship sailing the Atlantic Ocean but spent his early life in Virginia, near Madison Court House. Somehow, he learned to read before the war, although such knowledge was illegal in Virginia. He enlisted when he was 16 and came to Berea immediately after completing his army service, still in uniform. Rogers' Account Book notes that Burleigh was paid for labor April 17, 1866. In May, Burleigh paid his tuition. Throughout the remainder of 1866 and '67, Burleigh was being paid for work in the brickyard and using his wages to pay for his own board and books.[159]

In his *Journal* (June 28, 1866), Rogers recorded, "Angus Burleigh promised to be the Saviour's or rather prayed with me that the Lord would help him." In an American Missionary Association report, Rogers wrote: "Recently a colored young man [Burleigh] in the Academic department, of very great promise, has been led to trust in his Savior and has found sweet peace. He is from near Frankfort and very enthusiastic for the school." Burleigh joined Union Church September 22, 1866, having been baptized by John Rogers in Brushy Fork, and eventually became a trusted member of the congregation — on May 4, 1869, he was appointed member of a committee to confer with "leading colored brethren" concerning "their attendance upon their Christian duties at this church." Eventually, Burleigh was ordained as a Methodist Episcopal minister, held pastorates in Brooklyn, N.Y., Quincey, Illinois, and Milwaukee, Wisconsin, and served as chaplain of the Illinois State Senate. In addition to his ministerial positions, Burleigh taught at a colored school in Richmond, Indiana, where he was also principal in 1875-76. He maintained connections with Berea and friendship with Bereans throughout his long life.[160]

While he was a student at Berea, Burleigh seems to have been a favorite of both Fee and Rogers. Burleigh made rapid progress, and his teachers and sponsors took pride in his educational and spiritual growth — as an individual student, he was the sign that the whole experiment at Berea was workable: Burleigh's progress meant Berea really was the solution to the Camp Nelson problem.

When Fee traveled to raise funds in spring of 1867, he wrote Angus Burleigh from Pittsburgh (April 25, 1867) an encouraging and confidential letter, fatherly without being patronizing. Indeed, Fee was listed as Burleigh's guardian in 1869, the year Burleigh turned 21.[161]

Burleigh's recollections of his early student life constitute a priceless contribution to Berea's history. He recalled that in the spring of 1866, while he and thousands of other black soldiers waited to be mustered out of Camp Nelson, he met John G. Fee, who, according to Burleigh's testimony, "immediately" asked him to come to Berea. Apparently, Burleigh was one of many black soldiers at the camp Fee approached with his invitation. Burleigh remarks that his name was the forty-second in Fee's notebook. Burleigh started for Berea in April, 1866, and found on his arrival only three houses on the Ridge, including "...an old frame building where was displayed some cheap merchandise of all sorts," Rogers' house and Fee's house.[162]

The day after his arrival, Burleigh entered school, then still housed in the district schoolhouse: "it had two rooms — grammar & Primary

— Mr. Rogers & Miss Snedaker were the teachers." There were no black persons in higher grades, but Burleigh remembered that Miss Snedaker had two or three "little colored" children.[163]

Burleigh himself joined the grammar school students. "There was a holding of breath," he wrote, "and look of surprise around the room when I went in. Mr. Rogers gave me a seat in a corner by myself." Ten or twelve students were in the room, as Burleigh recalled, and some students did more than stare. Wheeler reported (November 22, 1866) that there was "another exodus of white students" after Burleigh's entrance.[164]

Angus Augustus Burleigh composed his *John G. Fee: Founder of Berea College* as a glowing personal tribute, but it is simply the most elaborate of the various eulogies which blacks of early Berea offered to Fee and to his memory. In Burleigh's work, Fee emerges clearly as a man with so much love for black people that he was enabled to actualize a vision of equality. Nothing struck Fee as inconceivable — it required some special grace for Fee to introduce grown men (ex-soldiers in uniform) into a gradeschool situation. Most people would have regarded adult blacks as ineligible for work in primary school, but Fee freely placed a 22-year-old black soldier alongside a six-year-old white girl. Fee was truly an egalitarian. When he wrote that Berea would accept *all* who were of good moral character, he meant *all*. For him the social roles and categories were meaningless beside the unity the gospel of Christ gave to the whole human race. But, perhaps more

Angus A. Burleigh when he was Berea's oldest living graduate, 1914.

Courtesy of Berea College Archives

striking than Fee's idealism was his practicality. He was willing to start where people were, wherever that was; he was willing to start small, with work that might have been regarded (and was) as meaningless or hopeless — teaching the ex-slave, now far past the accepted age for learning, to read, beginning at the very beginning.

Quoting Fee himself, who applied the verse to his own work again and again, Burleigh wrote, "We should not forget the day of small things." (Zechariah 4:10) The words represent Burleigh's epitaph for the man who had found him exactly at the juncture of slavery and freedom and encouraged him to possess his freedom fully.[165]

8. "Great blessings...to the African Race"

On May 2, 1866, writing from Lexington, Fee described a recruiting trip to Louisville, "to gather young soldiers (colored) just being mustered out. 31 have engaged to come immediately to school."[166]

Rogers, as school superintendent, filed a lengthy report with the American Missionary Association in June, 1866. At that time, the new school had been open for two completed terms. "There has been gain in outward things," he wrote,

> During the seven months since my return, eleven frame and two log houses, have been completed and commenced in and about Berea. Some of these buildings are small and some desirable. [This letter is badly blotted and has many indecipherable passages for that reason.]
>
> [Hanson has] a planing machine ordered and an additional saw mill, owned at Berea, erected three miles from there. A few white families have moved to the place, and more than a dozen *valuable* colored families. After Christmas, the time when contracts for labor usually expire in the state, we expect great numbers of colored people, indeed they are coming now continually. The most of these families are very desirable acquisitions to the colony, which will gather to it from the colored race the most energetic and those most desirous of the [blot]
>
> At one time there threatened to be a little friction. We work together, and go to church and school together as brethren, and I hope may even have such a measure of the blessing of God as to be of one heart.
>
> The school opened the first of Jan. Some weeks later when colored children began to attend the Primary Department, about half the white scholars left in both

Departments. The excitement was great and many in the community took sides against the mixed school.

The trials I am sure did [blot]

The last term which has just closed was a quiet and profitable one. Sixty seven pupils were in attendance if I remember aright, about half white. The prejudice has diminished very much, and the prospect for the future is very encouraging....We do not [?] a rapid so much as a healthful growth.

[blot]

It is a great joy to know the Inst. and community are regarded with such great favor by the colored people of that part of the state. The height of ambition with many is to get a home near Berea. The place itself is a comfort and a hope and encouragement to them. Some from distant parts of the state expect to be with us next term.

[blot]

The meetings held with the colored people in regions beyond us have been very cheering indeed. It is a cause of continued gratitude that the Holy Spirit is so moving upon that people. Bro Fee and myself desire to have meetings with them at Richmond, Lexington, Danville &c as soon as possible. We may make regular visits.

[blot]

I think Berea is to be a place from which great blessings are to flow and especially to the African race.[167]

In the *Birth of Berea: A Story of Providence*, Rogers explains that the first location of the school was near the old district schoolhouse, where a couple of "neat cottages" were constructed to house increasing number of students. What is now the main campus, some half-mile distant from the district building, was being cleared. Students, mostly blacks, were hired to cut down underbrush and superfluous trees and grub out stumps. This was "no small task," Rogers remarks, "but was gradually accomplished in the course of two or three years." The work was done by students, who were thus enabled to pay part of their school expenses.[168]

The first college classes at Berea represent patterns established in the community and the school for many years — the mingling of children of staff members (most frequently of Yankee origin), blacks and Appalachians became wholly characteristic of the institution. These diverse populations had, of course, been represented in Berea's development all along: in the postwar school, their relationship became institutionalized and official. In the community, these three groups lived and worshiped together. Most of Berea's students at this time were children of settlers, residents who had chosen to join the Berea Colony. Certainly this was true of the Yankee emigrants, true of families from Jackson County, Kentucky, who gathered near the College, and also true of the blacks. "The parents of most of the pupils residing in Berea," according to the 1867-68 Catalogue, "have come here to educate their children." At that time, most Berea students were black, and most of those black students belonged to families who had settled in Berea, with the intention of remaining.[169]

John G. Hanson's "saw and planing mills gave employment for many persons, and mechanics were needed for the new buildings, both of the college and the citizens." Many temporary buildings were thrown together in haste, dormitories and a rude chapel, "very rough and barn-like," which also served as school rooms with swinging partitions.[170]

"All the teachers," Rogers says, "were so busy they had hardly time to eat. Each new comer, whether student or citizen must be received and cared for. Work must be provided for all who wished to toil, with the axe or in the kitchen; those who had nothing to pay for tuition or books must be advised and encouraged to do all possible for themselves, meetings must be attended, and all those things done which pertain to a young and growing settlement."[171]

Yet the teachers seem to have been happy: Ellen P. T. Wheeler recalled the year as a "very prosperous & happy one for us all." She and her husband supervised the Boarding Hall for nearly 20 boarders, "nearly all colored young men." "At the close of the year," she wrote, "we had a 'grand commencement' in the grove around the old district school building & we had fine music, speeches, etc. etc."[172]

Elizabeth Rogers' memories of these years are less positive. Trying to rebuild their house, destroyed during the exile, the Rogers family felt compelled to move in before the outside walls were up "to protect it from fire and mob violence. Perhaps we were in greater danger after the war than before," she wrote, "the school had opened its doors to the colored people and we were threatened constantly by Ku Klux bands, or in danger from the reckless shooting of half-drunken southerners who rode up and down our streets at all hours."[173]

Berea must have then been a place of great excitement, in both positive and negative ways. An enormous social unheaval was taking place. Rogers describes a movement that would transform Berea for decades to come: "The coming of black people to Berea," Rogers wrote,

> for a time was phenomenal. Black Valley, a mile away from the college, swarmed with them, from the pickaninny to the old granny in the chimney corner. Berea was the land of promise, and to reach it, with all they had on

their backs, or at best in a rickety old cart, was the fulfillment of their hopes. To care for these grown-up, trusting children was a hard task and touched the hearts of the workers, and their pocketbooks as well. The men worked in the fields, the women washed for the folks on the "hill" and the aged and helpless were fed from pantries which were never overstocked.[174]

Elizabeth Rogers' descriptions of the same phenomena support her husband's observations:

> With the opening of the new Berea, the lately enfranchised colored people came flocking to us, claiming our help and protection, and it was no small part of the duty of the Faculty to establish those people in homes of their own and make them self-supporting. It was wonderful how quickly they became so, and how wisely on the whole they used their freedom. For many years the old and feeble men and women were pensioners on our bounty. I have seen our kitchen almost black with a crowd of old aunties who had stopped for "a cup of Miss Lizzie's coffee" and to beg a bit of white bread to carry home to the rheumatic husband or ailing children. To fill capacious pockets or baskets made large inroads upon our slender purses, but what could we do.

Her children, Mrs. Rogers stated, "used to be more eager for their tales of horror of old slave times than...for Hans Christian Andersen... and learned of Br'er Rabbit long before Joel Chandler Harris gave him to the world." When she took up teaching again, soon after the reopening, Mrs. Rogers employed a black woman (Louisa) to care for her children.[175]

"Our home was not built for ourselves alone," Elizabeth Rogers remarked,

> indeed sometimes I used to think our claims came last. Almost every teacher spent his first few days or weeks with us. The pilgrim weary and foot-sore from the mountains always had a welcome. The half timid colored man was never turned away. From the north came to us wise and celebrated men, who sat at our table and by our fireside. Our children did not need to go from home to see the world's people; they came to us.[176]

In all the emphasis upon blacks pouring into Berea, the white mountain people were not forgotten. Fee went to Jackson County in

August, 1866, and was pleased with what he found there. Because of the teaching and preaching of American Missionary workers (especially George Candee) in Jackson County, the region was fully "prepared." "Now there is a generation of men & women," Fee wrote, "educated to the principles of justice & mercy of righteousness."[177]

9. Third Term (September-November 1866): Berea — A Success

"The third term of the school is now in session," Fee wrote, "about half the school are colored. The issue of educating the two classes together has been fairly met and the people of the community have made up their minds. A majority of the white voters decided to give us trustees who were in favor of our using the district house for our mixed school, until we could erect buildings of our own." Fee reported that threats had been made against the school. "This...has intimidated many. This very malice in men is giving the place quite an advertisement." Still, the school and community continued to grow. Fee asked the American Missionary Association for $10,000 to buy land to sell in lots to black settlers. "We have access now to large congregations of these colored people in this and adjoining counties," Fee wrote. "The congregations of white people in Jackson county are very encouraging. There is an open door here that no man can shut."[178]

Willard W. Wheeler, in an official American Missionary Association report, wrote, "It has now become a settled point that those who come to this school are to recite in the same classes and share the same advantages as do others of whatever race."[179]

Wheeler's report continued very positively: "The advancement of the pupils has been marked. Many who could scarcely read at all 6 months ago are now studying arithmetic, writing and are through the second reader. Thus much and more has been done inside the school house, outside the change has been even more marked." Two substantial school buildings had been erected, a church was being financed and planned; Wheeler asked for money for the boarding hall and the church, and money to buy up land from those who were "not friendly." He said he had not "the slightest doubt but that [they] could sell one hundred [small lots] before Christmas 1867."[180]

The greatest change seemed to Wheeler to have occurred in the people, black and white. "It is very surprising," he said,

> to witness the spirit of improvement which has taken possession of the people. Old briar fields are being cleaned up and greater activity manifested in all branches of business. Within the last 14 months 26 families have

moved into the place, or near enough to send their children to school....In the adjoining counties, particularly Jackson and Estill, Berea is very popular and the presence of colored children is considered no bar to their sending their children. Want of means is all that keeps hundreds away.[181]

Thus, within a few months of reopening, Berea was developing in amazing and fruitful ways. To Fee and some others it was a dream come true.

During this period, Fee usually divided his time between Berea and Camp Nelson, but he was confined to Berea through much of the third term of 1866, because his son Burritt was seriously ill, and Fee insisted on nursing the young man himself. Fee's ideas about the new project, ideas clarified and strengthened by his experiences of two unique racial situations, were both humane and practical. "They [the blacks]," he wrote, "to [attain?] highest development must not remain a nation of boot blacks or mere stevedores. They must become owners of land and producers of valuable commodities. Then they will be esteemed in their own eyes and in the eyes of others."[182]

The whole business of land ownership and settlement engaged much of Fee's attention: "I would avoid aggregating in our county or part of the state," he said. "[rather] have groups all over the state (interspersed with as many good whites as would go in) so as to sustain a school & church. Give lands & education — then prejudice will readily give way." He wanted a land company formed in Ohio to aid in this project, because

> most white men here [in Kentucky] who have two to four hundred acres will not sell a scrap to a "nigger."
>
> But friends of the colored man will & then so arrange sale of lots as to have them in community so as to have for them schools & churches.
>
> Someone may say 'let the colored man alone — let him find his own way' — why not then dispense with educational efforts for him. I do not propose to feed him but put an axe & land within his reach & let him work out his salvation — help him to a home.[183]

Fee's proposal, while it received no particular attention in the country at large, was fully enacted in Berea. The flood of black settlers arrived in part because land *was* available in Berea — farms and town lots, with many white neighbors sworn to help them. From the beginning, Berea's educational experiment depended upon the broader social experiment in the whole community: Berea College began in the framework of Berea Colony — and certainly the school's initial success was altogether due to the social and religious context built for it.

On December 12, 1866, Fee wrote again to the American Missionary Association concerning the need for land for black people "who have not as yet means with which to purchase and some white men who wish education for their children." The year — Berea's first year as an interracial institution — was ending. Fee wrote his estimation of what had been accomplished and what still needed to be done:

> Our school is a success — it is growing as fast as we can possibly find shelter for families & students. All is quiet & harmonious here. This is what many, North & South, did not expect.
>
> The people need a *demonstration* of capacity to study and *study together harmoniously* — just as they did a demonstration of capacity to *fight* & *work* & *live orderly. We are making that demonstration.*
>
> Many colored people have been afraid to come lest they too would be overwhelmed in the threatened ruin — so with many white families. When these shall see that other white children can be educated along with colored children and yet be intelligent, refined & efficient, then they will bring in their children; for they are now seeing that children are not to have respectability because "daddy has some land & niggers" but because children have character & brains.
>
> Our school ought not to be a crippled 'one hoss' affair — it ought to have building so good & facilities so great as to make the whole affair respectable & efficient.[184]

Rogers filed a report with the American Missionary Association as superintendent of Berea on December 20, 1866; "One of the best results of the school," he wrote, "is the great encouragement it has given to the colored people in this region...."[185]

In 1868, Fee reported that Berea Literary Institution had over 300 students, almost two-thirds of them black. "The School," he wrote, "is harmonious in an eminent degree." All who attend, he said, know that they must conform to the anti-caste rule or leave. "We seek to make this a matter of Christian *privilege* rather than a legal duty," Fee explained, "We teach that when Christ Jesus took upon him human nature, he dignified the nature of every man." That man, every room at the Berea school was full, and many students were "so desirous...for knowledge that they [were] willing to crawl up into low attics and there endure cold and privation."[186]

James H. Fairchild attended Berea's graduation exercises in 1868, held in a grove on the college grounds under a specially constructed bower. People came from the mountains and the Bluegrass "to the number of twelve hundred" and listened attentively all day. Before noon "orations, essays, and declamations" were delivered — of the 26 students who participated, "fourteen were reputed white and twelve colored," but Fairchild was unable to "divide them properly."

In the afternoon, visiting speakers, presumably Fairchild among them, addressed the crowd. He remarked that he was impressed "with the moral power and efficiency of the movement." To the outward eye, Berea had barely begun — "the buildings [were] temporary and the original forest [overshadowed] everything," but, on another level, Fairchild said, "it looked like a successful solution of the problem [of] 'impartial education' in the South."

The President of Oberlin College then remarked, "The spirit and tone of the place reminded me very much of the early days of Oberlin. If I mistake not, it is the beginning of great things."[187]

He was not mistaken.

In a report for 1869, Colonel Benjamin P. Runkle, Assistant Commissioner of the Freedmen's Bureau for Kentucky, described Berea College for General Oliver Otis Howard. This "outside" view of Berea provides crucial insights into the institution as it existed. To Berea, Runkle said, come "the sons and daughters upon whom the curse of slavery weighed more heavily than on any other class, the White Mountaineers of Kentucky." For this class, he maintained, neither the state and national governments nor the benevolent societies of the United States had made provision. He also thought Berea would "be of great importance to the colored people of Kentucky" — although that seems to have been a lesser concern to him.

At Berea, the commissioner saw "managers" who were "honest and trustworthy," who believed in God and loved their fellow men. "I never saw men working under such difficulties," he wrote, "and I never saw men with such faith...."

Runkle had attended a gathering of students in the chapel which he called "one of the most singular sights I ever witnessed...all shades and colors, all ages and conditions and all intent on one object, to escape from the bonds of ignorance." Accommodations for the scholars were crowded and uncomfortable. Students lived "in little rooms or dens, called attics." They were poor, "living upon nearly nothing, and working between time to pay for it." Runkle had observed "two bright, intelligent white boys" waiting on a table where both white and black students were seated. "And this they did cheerfully," he exclaimed, "for six cents an hour in order to get money to pay their board." He had heard one of the same white students read Latin and had found the young man "had opinions of his own." Runkle had seen "white girls sitting in the same class with black ones." It seemed to him that "it must have cost these young people a terrible struggle to come to this." He interviewed three black men, former soldiers, who had been at Berea for two years, and "intended to remain there six more."

He met Elizabeth Rogers and found her "a lady...fit to adorn any place in society." There she was, "living by no means surrounded by luxury, far out in that wild, mountain country, taking care of her family, providing for her boarders (for everybody [in Berea] takes in boarders) and teaching a number of these poor people besides." Ruckles was struck with wonder: "I have not seen many such people," he wrote.

In fact, he stated he had never seen anything like Berea before and never expected to see anything like it again. He concluded by advising General Oliver O. Howard of the Freedmen's Bureau to give Berea all the money the institution needed.[188]

10. 1870: The Fourth Annual Commencement of Berea College

June 29, 1870 — an audience of between 1,000-2,000, "about equal numbers of white and colored, intermingled without constraint." Morning exercises: orations by young men, freshmen and sophomores, and essays read by young ladies. Several students had been slaves. "When one of them, a young lady...alluded to her former condition, she sent...a thrill through the audience...." Afternoon exercises: addresses by the faculty and Judge William C. Goodloe of Lexington.

The college was "growing continually in public estimation" and the community around the college gradually increasing. Berea College was selling village lots to settlers for $100, farm land at rates of $15 to $40 per acre, and the institution solicited "families desiring to live in such an atmosphere and educate their children at an institution [with] excellent facilities for a thorough and accurate scholarship, under Christian influences."

"We have no more feeling of unrest [in Berea now]," Rogers wrote, "than if we were in the heart of New England."[189]

III. THE PRACTICAL ACHIEVEMENT

1. Fairchild's Administration, 1869-89

The year Edward Henry Fairchild began his administration as president of Berea College (1869) was an auspicious one, with Howard Hall (named for Oliver Otis Howard) being erected by the Freedmen's Bureau and the whole school settling into a kind of stability it had never known before. During the first decade of the reopened school (1866-75), "61 percent of the students were black, a proportion that remained constant throughout the Fairchild era."[190]

"Integration" during Fairchild's administration "went beyond the classroom. Both races sang in the choir, played on the football and baseball teams, belonged to the same literary societies, played in the band, sat indiscriminately in chapel, and ate in the same boarding halls." Certainly Fairchild deserves much of the credit for Berea's survival during this crucial period — amidst a hostile environment, the school flourished "without compromising its principles." But John G. Fee was President of the Board of Trustees of Berea College throughout Fairchild's administration, and his influence was incalculable. Like Fee, "Fairchild was not afraid to endorse social equality by name, and he practiced it in his home, where black servants and workmen as well as students and clergymen were guests at his table."[191]

In the 1870's, Fairchild wrote that "the most serious collision" he remembered happening between the races "was where an uncultured white girl complained that a colored girl called her 'poor white trash' and the colored girl replied that she did not do it till she called her 'Jigger.'" This controversy, Fairchild claimed, "was settled without difficulty." In fact, he said, "No school in the State [was] easier governed than [Berea]."[192]

During his administration, Berea became a "respected four-year college." His own estimation of the early years of his tenure in the presidency appears in *Berea College, Ky.: An Interesting History* (published 1883). The college achieved a degree of financial and staffing stability in the 1870's and 80's, and many new buildings were erected. But the great achievement was in social relations. Fairchild wrote that Berea College sought to eliminate prejudice or caste feeling,

> through its students, who carry the principles and feelings here imbibed to all parts of the country; by the constant exhibition of perfect equality and perfect harmony to all visitors, and especially to thousands at our annual commencements; by lectures, addresses and sermons of professors and advanced students, to colored, and white, and mixed audiences, gathered for religious, political, or educational purposes; and through the medium of the press.

Summing up Berea's position, Fairchild stated: Only "co-education [integrated education]...can secure the mutual regard, confidence and honorable deportment which must exist between these races, if we are to have a peaceful, intelligent and virtuous community."[193]

2. The Ku Klux Klan

Berea's early achievements came in the face of much external hostility. Activities of the Ku Klux Klan in Madison County from 1866-70 seem to have been extensive. With his characteristic minimizing touch, Rogers reports, "The Ku Klux Klan or the coarse jeers of drunken, hostile men and the careless firing of their pistols through the streets and the whizzing of bullets sometimes dangerously near did not often produce any permanent fear." Actually, the Bereans came to believe their opponents were afraid of *them*, fearful of doing them harm, holding them in "superstitious regard." Fee's enemies had a disconcerting way of dying violently, and the Berea abolitionists seemed always to reappear, stronger than ever.[194]

However, the father of one of the black children who integrated Berea in 1866 was murdered by the Ku Klux Klan, and Willard W. Wheeler was almost killed by a Klan mob in Lexington, which attacked him while he was on a business trip for Berea College. "For a year or two, about 1870 and later," Fairchild wrote, "the country was completely under [the Klan's] control. There was no protection for anybody against whom their violence was directed."[195]

The Rogers' son Raphael, recalling the days of his youth, wrote:

> For four years [1867-71] the lives of Mr. Fee and my Father were in more or less danger. On several occassions

[sic] to prevent the school buildings being fired armed pickets patrolled around them all night. For years when my Father was away at night my mother had us all sleep on the first floor on cots rather than in our bedrooms upstairs so that if the house were fired in the night we could be gotten out quickly. The anxiety was more intense at times than at others, but it was there for years. I have heard the bullets sing into our yard to strike the trees several times fired by drunken men at the house.

These dangers were incurred simply because of the anti-caste principle of the school, a principle for which Fee and Rogers were willing, Raphael wrote, "to imperil a great school, and their own lives & the lives of their families...." In Raphael Rogers' eyes — from his early teenage years, and then forever after — his father and Fee were "heroes defending at all risks a noble, righteous & glorious principle." The perils of attending Berea College may have given an incalculable depth to the education of Berea students in the early years. Raphael Rogers wrote, "...Some things were burned into my soul from the age of ten to fourteen which I am not likely to forget...."[196]

Education for blacks, whether integrated or not, was met with determined and violent opposition in Kentucky and throughout the South in the late 1860's. Reverend Abisha Scofield had been mobbed and driven out of Camp Nelson for superintending a black school. In March, 1868, John Rogers reported, "A house near Kirksville [a town in Madison County near Berea] which the colored people rented for school purposes and where they intended starting a school, was a few days ago burned." Some teachers at Freedmen's Bureau Schools were "insulted, threatened, ostracized, and even flogged or forcibly exiled," during this period. Schools which involved white teachers and black students were most violently opposed. "Of the 165 teachers [of blacks] remaining in Kentucky in August 1868, only twenty-one were white and they were located in towns where they might be protected. The reports of the Kentucky Superintendent of Education of 1868 contains a two page enumeration of outrages, threats, beatings and burnings." On January 1, 1869, John Watson Alvord reported to the Freedmen's Bureau, "...old prejudices remain, equality of rights is, more or less, resisted and the education of the freedmen, throughout most of the southern states receives as yet too little practical encouragement."[197]

The Ku Klux Klan was active in central Kentucky throughout this period. Blacks convened in Frankfort in 1871, having drawn up a list of 116 outrages by organized bands in Kentucky from November, 1867, to February, 1871.[198]

Yet by 1870, Berea College possessed property valued at $45,000, employed 11 teachers to teach 250 pupils, with boarding accommodations for 100. Fee's church at Berea had a membership of 151, with 232 attending Sunday School.[199]

Berea's achievement from 1866-1870, which must be measured in more than numbers, should be seen in its context of the opposition, prejudice and violence of that time — in Kentucky and the entire southern United States. Perhaps the total effect of organized lawlessness in and around Berea was more positive than negative, however, making the Berea community more closely knit. Rogers states, "The necessity of much coercive discipline on the part of the teachers was...diminished by the pressure from without. It has been said that the college paid little attention to lawless bands riding through the place and other marks of opposition, but this was because it had a great work on its hands, and could not stop long enough to be greatly disturbed by any ordinary dangers." He narrates a story of "seeing a person riding along the street nearest Howard Hall, a dormitory accommodating eighty students, draw a revolver and fire shots at the building where students were sitting at the open windows. Efforts to arrest and punish these trespassers were usually unavailing." This opposition, Rogers maintains, "was such as to bind all Bereans closer to each other."[200]

3. The Cooper Institute Meetings

Although much of its strength came from internal cohesion, Berea had already achieved national recognition: the close-knit community in central Kentucky was supported by a larger network of reformers and philanthropists in the North and East. The Cooper Institute meeting on Berea, when a number of famous men addressed the public in New York City concerning the new college's achievement and potential, took place in January, 1869, and such speakers as Horace Greeley and Henry Ward Beecher extolled Berea from the platform — the favorable publicity accruing to Berea was immense and eventually led to the donation of thousands of dollars.

Berea was praised most highly for its unique interracial experiment in education. Dr. Joseph Parrish Thompson said, for example, "That feature of this institution which especially commends itself to my confidence is that it is a school for the training of men without reference to race. It is a school which in its fundamental principle overrules distinctions of caste and brings together men and women to receive knowledge from the same fountain — guidance from the same teachers. The principle of equality, the principle of fraternity, this

Integrated club at Berea College: a football team, ca. 1900. *Courtesy of Berea College Archives*

Integrated club at Berea College: Utile Dulce Literary Society, ca. 1900. *Courtesy of Berea College Archives*

recognition of simple manhood was begun long ago in this institution, before the war....[201]

Reverend Richard Salter Storrs spoke more specifically of the same achievement:

> I do not believe that any of us really think how much has been attained in simply solving [the] question of combining whites and blacks in the same institution, sitting side by side on the same benches, studying out of the same text books, on Southern soil. We have been meditating over that question year after year, how that thing was to be done, and these men have gone and done it. They have actually done the thing, and blacks and whites are studying under the same roof. Berea College has solved the problem and solved it in the right way.[202]

Reverend Howard Crosby remarked, "Berea College has gone through that severe ordeal which makes it a strong institution. On that account we ought to give it our earnest sympathy and our hearty help. Then it is in the right place. It is Kentucky curing Kentucky."[203]

The Cooper Institute speeches marked the wide public recognition of Berea's greatest achievement: the actualization of Fee's brilliant scheme for interracial education. It was brilliant, because it was simple. While others argued and debated, while a whole nation resisted and protested, while the wise and prudent counselled moderation, while the conventionally pious took refuge in their conventional piety, the Bereans — under Fee's leadership — simply *did* it. They got the thing done: blacks and whites studying together under the same roof, living and working together in the same community, worshipping together in the same church. It was a staggering accomplishment.

4. The Issue of Intermarriage

In June, 1872, Fairchild, writing to the American Missionary Association, asked advice of that group concerning the following question:

> If the two students of suitable age, one white and the other colored, should become engaged to be married, and should conduct themselves with as much propriety as discreet young people usually do under such circumstances, ought we to sever their connexion with the school on that account?

He requested that each leader of the American Missionary Association answer the question separately, without consulting the others. His own mind, he said, was "clear on the subject." But, he confessed, "I have sometimes found myself wrong when I was clear."[204]

An actual incident had apparently precipitated Fairchild's question, even though he said they had no such case *yet*. Fee wrote to E. M. Cravath less than a week later, with a much more intense set of questions. Cravath was unable to attend the next trustees' meeting, a meeting in which the question of interracial dating and marriage for Berea College students would be considered. Fee wrote:

> In view of what you understand to be right in the sight of God — the example of Jesus Christ and the declared position of Berea College as set forth in her constitution — that the position of the institution — the action of its officers shall be "anticaste" — are you ready as one to reaffirm that in the treatment of our students in their social relations *we will treat white as colored & colored as white & make no distinction on account of color?* Please answer.

It is sufficiently obvious what answer Fee was demanding.

He went on, however, to clarify and qualify (to some extent) his expectations:

> I do not ask that you shall decide that everyone colored or white who shall ask to go with the opposite color shall be allowed to do so.
> 1. He or she may be of doubtful virtue. He or she may be reckless — desire to do some indiscreet thing — go to Richmond where it [would] not be wise to do so. But when a young white man like J. F. Gregg [Fee's own cousin John Fee Gregg, who seems to have actually begun 'dating' a black girl], of Christian character, of good family — a first class young man of rare virtue, thinking it would be right that he should go to one of our monthly lectures with a young lady, so near white as that the difference is not greater than between my wife & myself, and to a place where we allow our young men to go with young ladies, would you say the reason is simply that one is colored & the other white, therefore they should not walk together. This has been done by a young lady acting as temporary lady principal [evidently Mrs. Juliet C. Clark].
> The question before our Faculty is what reply shall we give to her. We have reason to believe that a majority of our faculty will sustain her action — will not say her deci-

sion was wrong — the matter may go to the trustees. You may go away soon — I know not.

Can you say to me as President of that Board & through me to the board *"Make no distinction on the mere ground of color."* In case of immorality, indiscretion &c. make discriminations & restrictions, but not on ground of color.[205]

The trustees followed Fee's lead and passed a rule permitting interracial dating, "if no obstacle but simply that of complexion exists...." Even "intermarriage was not forbidden, but the faculty in its function *in loco parentis* should warn the parties 'of dangers to which they will expose themselves and their parents' and should discourage betrothal while students were still in school." The new "Social Relations" rule states clearly, "...The mere fact that persons of different colors are engaged to be married is not sufficient cause for removing them [from school], provided they conduct themselves with appropriate discretion...." As James McPherson remarks, this policy was "remarkably liberal...for that time and place." However, the only interracial marriage recorded for a Berea student from this period occurred between John T. Robinson and one of Fee's cousins.[206]

This decision, one of Fee's last major policy-making breakthroughs, represents the consistency and thoroughness of his thinking on racial issues. Although Fee's reaction to having John Robinson marry into his family is not on record, we may assume that Fee approved. In the hundreds of letters which Fee wrote, no evidence indicates any inconsistency in his attitude toward blacks. He proclaimed and practiced equality. Racism simply had no place in his thinking or behavior. In 1874, at the Reunion Convention of Abolitionists in Chicago (their Jubilee), Fee warned the assembly that "neither the spirit of bondage nor that of caste discrimination had been eradicated and that the abolitionists' tasks did not end until these ills were finally buried."[207]

5. Fee's Achievement

Fee's opposition to injustice and prejudice, his dedication to "a practical recognition of the brotherhood of man," never resulted in total success. What vision of peace and justice has ever done so? Yet John G. Fee is a figure of the magnitude of Gandhi or Martin Luther King: a man of singular moral and spiritual stature, of courage and compassion, who dedicated his life to a great cause and taught, encouraged, exhorted and led others to do the same. He has scarcely been granted his place in history, yet his work with interracial education at Berea, his insightful and humane proposals for social harmony between the races (ideas which put him a hundred years ahead of his time) and his heroic struggle at Camp Nelson surely deserve careful notice.

Local Berea people still speak of the founder of their town as "Old Fee" in a tone of derision. Students and staff at the college he founded frequently scoff at the mention of his name, indulging some vague notion that he was a religious fanatic whose only concern was baptism by immersion. A prominent Richmond lawyer informed me recently that "Fee was nothing but a troublemaker anyway." Fee was hated and dismissed in his time because of his stand against slavery and for equality of all races. An historical explanation of why his memory should be hated and dismissed *now* is not within the purview of this work. Some people have no idea what he accomplished, and others have no notion of the importance of his mission.

People in his own day were much more aware of Fee's great achievements. John T. Robinson, a black student who was graduated from Berea in 1874, wrote to Fee later expressing sentiments that many black people must have shared:

> I used to stop and look at you & think how you must have enjoyed witnessing that which you had prayed and worked for so long — namely a living demonstration of the brotherhood of mankind, and I can safely say that all of those *old students* will always *love* and *revere you* through all time as they would a father and the profitable lessons you have taught us both by precept and example will always be treasured up as the true idea of manhood, and the *ends* of life....[208]

In the same letter, Robinson states that the blacks of Berea knew Fee as "their only true advocate."

In his own day, Fee received — at least from fellow abolitionists — some fitting recognition. At the annual meeting of the American Missionary Association for 1869 (reported in December), Fee was present as a hero "From the Front," one of the "men who [had] emphatically borne the heat and burden of the day." The reporter of the meeting stated, "It was particularly refreshing to see the healthy, happy face of Mr. Fee and to get a chat with him about the old days, when Kentucky mobs used to assail him and threaten his life, and it was good to hear him speak, and note how much life and vigor are still left to him." The assembly concluded with a pentecostal meeting for prayer, General Oliver Otis Howard presiding. "The atmosphere was like benediction," the reporter said, "assuring us of the approbation of God."

"Let us all kneel as we pray," said the Christian soldier Howard:

> So on their knees they fell. John G. Fee, a veteran hero in our work...delivered from prisons and from death in times agone, has come to jubilee. Like a giant in the faith, with soul too full for utterance he rolls off his burdens at the foot of the throne. So on they prayed till the hour was spent....[209]

It is appropriate that our last glimpse of John G. Fee should be at this point in his life, his apotheosis, with all his achievement clear, appreciated and revered — on his knees to be lifted up by the prayers of men who respected and loved him. He had his great moment. And his dedicated life changed the world, in ways we can hardly estimate. The college he founded, the community he established, testify still — however imperfectly — to the vision of one godly and practical man who saw human equality as a reality we must all recognize and an ideal we must strive for. Early Berea remains — even though we can point to the date of its "failure" — an achievement we must emulate. For awhile it worked — in spite of everything, it worked! Those years of Berea's success as an interracial community are a reproach still to the racism and inequality of our society. And a challenge.

A white student who attended Berea in the days of the interracial experiment later wrote: "The scoffers who would say that whites and blacks cannot associate on terms of absolute scholastic equality, with mutual respect, genuine friendship, and absence of any harmful consequences, have not proved their contention for...all of the above things have actually existed at Berea."[210]

APPENDIX

Camp Nelson: Reverend Abisha Scofield and Reverend Gabriel Burdett

The village of Ariel at Camp Nelson, and the church and school, continued in existence for many years. The village had been established on land purchased by John G. Fee in 1868 (after an "arduous time") and parcelled out to black purchasers. The church, founded by Fee in September, 1864, was maintained under the ministry of Gabriel Burdett, long after Fee's departure. In 1871, his church at Camp Nelson had 191 members, with 200 in the Sunday School. Ariel Academy was partially sponsored at first by the Freedmen's Bureau, which in the spring of 1868 bought for the academy buildings once part of the school complex built for the refugees when Camp Nelson was a military operation. The Bureau's purchase, for $1,520, included a large boarding house, with wings suitable for a schoolhouse and chapel. Apparently, the institution operating in this structure, the school founded by Fee for Camp Nelson refugees, simply continued through the change of ownership. In 1871, Ariel Academy's property was assessed at $2,000 — two teachers were employed, with 100 pupils attending. Trustees of Ariel Academy included John G. Fee and Gabriel Burdett. For many years, the American Missionary Association supplied workers for Ariel, superintended by Fee's son, Howard. The charter of Camp Nelson was exactly like Berea's, according to Fee. When Fee made his will, the church and academy at Camp Nelson were still in operation, but in 1901 (the year of his death), the Camp Nelson work was near failure. In 1902, the trustees of the school at Camp Nelson "made overtures" to Berea College — evidently Ariel Academy was in need of financial support and students — and its trustees wished their institution to become part of Berea. Ariel's trustees wanted their institution to become the repository for Berea's black students if the Day Law should be passed. Given Camp Nelson's history, such a move would not have been unreasonable, and some

Berea trustees supported it. (Fee to Smith, Apr 9, 1868; Rogers to Frost 21 Nov 1901.)

Reverend Abisha Scofield remained at Camp Nelson after Fee departed, only to be driven out by a murderous mob in 1866. A New Yorker, Scofield visited Berea in 1865 to consider the possibility of moving there, but eventually he returned to his native state, where his grown children lived. Asked by Fee to serve as a financial agent for Berea, Scofield replied — regretfully — that he and his family were so poor that he seemed "compelled to *dig* rather than to *beg.*" A trustee of Berea for only one year, Scofield probably never attended a meeting; like others, he was asked to show up or resign — and he resigned. (Scofield to Fee 4 May 1869 BCA.)

Reverend Gabriel Burdett, the first black to serve on Berea's board and surely one of the first Negroes — if not the first — to hold such a position in the American South, was born a slave in Garrard County, December 13, 1829. Burdett was owned by a distant cousin of Morgan Burdett, a white Berea College trustee who served on the board at the same time as Gabriel. While he was still in his twenties, Gabriel Burdett became a slave preacher, given authority by the white congregation to hold services among the blacks at Forks of Dick's River Baptist Church in Garrard County, the church in which all white Burdetts were members. Gabriel was permitted to use the church on Sunday afternoon for his "people of color." In 1862, he was brought before the church and reprimanded strongly for intemperate language used toward the church ("doubtless," says Forrest Calico, "on account of his desire for freedom for himself and others of his race"). In 1869, after years of absence, he was excluded for non-attendance. Many slaves (at least 14) named Burdett belonged to the church which Gabriel pastored in Garrard County, although by the end of the Civil War most of them, like their black minister, had left the congregation. (Forrest Calico, *History of Garrard County, Kentucky, and Its Churches* [New York: Hobson Book Press, 1947], pp. 307, 313, 317, 318, 320-22, 333, 336, 337, 347.)

Burdett enrolled in the Union Army July 15, 1864, and served in Company "I," 114th Regiment U.S. Colored Infantry Volunteers, as a private. He was "on detached duty at Camp Nelson, Ky." from November 30, 1860, to May 3, 1865, then sent to Nashville October 31, 1865, where he served until August 31, 1866, honorably discharged (in Nashville) September 15, 1866. During part of his army service, Burdett acted as Fee's assistant, a minister, nurse and teacher at Camp Nelson. With Fee, he labored to help the families of Camp Nelson soldiers. Because of his efforts there, white camp official Thomas Butler (manager of the camp's United States Sanitary Commission station) described Burdett as "a noble and extraordinary man." Certainly the description must be apt, for Burdett's own letters, to Fee and others, reveal an unaffected wisdom and piety which epitomized the virtue Fee perceived in ex-slaves in general. Perhaps he had seen it most clearly in Gabriel Burdett. (Gabriel Burdett Civil War Pension File, WC 786-792 in National Archives. Gutman, *Black Family*. p. 372; *Report of the Adjutant General*, II, 59.)

As a preacher, Burdett won Fee's highest praise, and he served as pastor of the Church of Christ at Camp Nelson, which Fee had founded, for many years after Fee's permanent removal to Berea. In 1870, Burdett wrote to the American Missionary Association, stating that he had been regular pastor of Camp Nelson's church since March, 1867. "The colored people in this state," he wrote, "were once all members of the white slave holding churches until we were emancipated were merely governed altogether by them their pride and predices [sic] and even now this is the only independent church in all of the land accept [sic] the Churches that were independent before the war like that of Berea and kindred churches. And I have never been able to see how we could be independent without coming out entiley [sic] from all of the old slaveholding churches...." (Burdett to Cravath, 2 Nov 1870 AMA 44678.)

In January, 1867, Burdett was staying with Fee in Berea, and considering leaving Camp Nelson to bring his family to Berea to be educated, while he traveled as an evangelist. E. M. Cravath, whom Burdett had met in Nashville, advised Burdett to take this step. But Burdett got an unexpected chance to buy land at Camp Nelson the next month; having a place of his own there may have helped him decide against Berea. By May, 1867, Burdett had returned to Camp Nelson permanently, reporting to the American Missionary Association that he had been teaching the district school there and had reorganized the church and school where Scofield had been. (Fee to Whipple 25 Jan 1867 AMA 44413; Burdett to Smith 21 May 1867 AMA 44462.)

One of Gabriel Burdett's numerous children, John G. Burdett (born March 20, 1867), was named to honor one of Gabriel Burdett's most important relationships: with John G. Fee at Camp Nelson. (Burdett's Pension File.)

Howard Hall, built in 1869 by the Freedman's Bureau.
Courtesy of Berea College Archives

NOTES

[1] Herbert G. Gutman, *The Black Family in Slavery and Freedom 1750-1925* (New York: Pantheon Books, 1976), p. 370.

[2] Fee to Simeon S. Jocelyn 12 July 1864 in American Missionary Association Archives, item no. 44007, on Fisk University microfilm in Hutchins Library, Berea College; all subsequent references appear abbreviated as AMA followed by an item number.

[3] AMA 44007.

[4] *Ibid.*; John Gregg Fee, *Autobiography of John G. Fee* (Chicago: National Christian Association, 1891), p. 175.

[5] *Ibid.*

[6] *Ibid.*

[7] *Ibid.*

[8] Fee to Jocelyn 18 July 1864 AMA 44008.

[9] *Ibid.*

[10] *Ibid.*

[11] *Ibid.*

[12] Gutman, p. 371.

[13] *Freedom: A Documentary History of Emancipation: (Series III) The Black Military Experience*, ed. Ira Berlin (New York: Cambridge U. Press, 1982),

p. 195. Kentucky slaveowners' mistreatment of the wives and children of slave soldiers is well-documented. See, for example, the affidavit of a Kentucky black soldier's widow, filed at Camp Nelson 25 Mar 1865. *Black Military Experience.* p. 268.

[14] Gutman, p. 372; Lewis and Richard H. Collins, *History of Kentucky* (Berea: Kentucke Imprints, 1976), II, 139.

[15] Joel M. Partridge Student File, Oberlin Alumni Records; Fee to Michael E. Strieby 1 Aug 1864 AMA 44015.

[16] Fee to Jocelyn 8 Aug 1864 AMA 44016-44019.

[17] *Ibid.*

[18] *Ibid.;* Victor B. Howard, *Black Liberation in Kentucky: Emancipation and Freedom 1862-1884* (Lexington: U. Press of Kentucky, 1983), p. 119.

[19] Fee to George Whipple 22 Aug 1864 AMA 44023.

[20] Fee to Whipple 27 Aug 1864 AMA 44027; Fee to Strieby 29 Aug 1864 AMA 44030.

[21] Fee to Strieby 10 Sept 1864 AMA 44035.

[22] Fee to Strieby 22 Sept 1864 AMA 44038.

[23] Scofield to Strieby 1 Oct 1864 AMA 44040; *Black Military Experience.* p. 715; Laurence Jacob Friedman, *Gregarious Saints: Self and Community in American Abolitionism, 1830-1870* (New York: Cambridge U. Press, 1982), pp. 97, 107.

[24] Fee to Partridge, 16 Sept 1864 BCA; Fee to Strieby 7 Oct 1864 AMA 44045; Fee to Whipple 10 Oct 1864 AMA 44048. One of the small children who entered the Berea School when Laura Fee was in charge recalled his first teacher over 60 years later. *Berea Citizen.* 20 Oct 1927.

[25] AMA 44048.

[26] Scofield to Strieby 1 Nov 1864 AMA 44052; Fee to Strieby 11 Nov 1864 AMA 44054.

[27] Fee to Whipple 26 Nov 1864 AMA 44057.

[28] Gutman, pp. 372, 373; *Black Military Experience.* p. 717; Scofield to Strieby 1 Dec 1864 AMA 44059.

[29] *Black Military Experience.* pp. 715-717. The fact that the expulsion from Camp Nelson lasted three days probably explains the discrepancy in accounts of the incident concerning its date. T. E. Hall reported that the incident occurred on or about November 20.

[30] Gutman, p. 373.

[31] AMA 44059. In July, 1864, Gen. George Thomas had ordered all black dependents turned out from posts and camps and "their masters informed of their expulsion. Ejection of black families constituted in effect their return to slavery." *Black Military Experience.* p. 195.

[32] T. E. Hall to Elnathan Davis 14 Dec 1864 AMA 44061.

[33] *Black Military Experience.* p. 716.

[34] Gutman, p. 374; AMA 44061.

[35] AMA 44061.

[36] Scofield to Strieby 9 Dec 1864 AMA 44060.

[37] *Ibid.*

[38] AMA 44061; John Vetters to Scofield 16 Dec 1864 AMA 44062.

[39] Howard, *Black Liberation.* p. 118; Fee to Whipple 2 Jan 1865 AMA 44064.

[40] AMA 44064; Gutman, p. 374; *Black Military Experience.* p. 718.

⁴¹Fee to Whipple 10 Jan 1865 AMA 44070; Howard, *Black Liberation,* p. 119.
⁴²Gabriel Burdett to Fee 20 Jan 1865 AMA 44071.
⁴³Fee to Whipple 3 Feb 1865 AMA 44073; Scofield to AMA 4 Feb 1865 AMA 44075.
⁴⁴Fee to Whipple 7 Feb 1865 AMA 44076-44077.
⁴⁵*Ibid.*
⁴⁶*Ibid.*
⁴⁷Fee to Whipple 8 Feb 1865 AMA 44079-44082.
⁴⁸Fee to Whipple 9 Feb 1865 AMA 44086.
⁴⁹Fee to Tappan 21 Feb 1865 AMA 44091.
⁵⁰Howard, *Black Liberation,* p. 117; Fee to Whipple 9 Feb 1865 AMA 44086; Fee to Tappan 21 Feb 1865 AMA 44901.
⁵¹Fee to Whipple 21 Feb 1865 AMA 44093.
⁵²*Ibid.*
⁵³Fee to Whipple 25 Feb 1865 AMA 44097.
⁵⁴Fee to Whipple 21 Feb 1865 AMA 44093.
⁵⁵*American Missionary,* Vol. IX, no. 6 (June 1865), p. 121.
⁵⁶Scofield to Strieby 3 Mar 1865 AMA 44104; Fee to Strieby 7 Mar 1865 AMA 44106.
⁵⁷AMA 44106.
⁵⁸Fee to Whipple 15 Mar 1865 AMA 44112; Fee to Whipple 24 Mar 1865 AMA 44116.
⁵⁹AMA 44116; Elnathan Davis to Strieby 1 Apr 1865 AMA 44119; Fee to Strieby 21 Apr 1865 AMA 44112.
⁶⁰AMA 44419; AMA 44122.
⁶¹Fee to Strieby 2 May 1865 AMA 44126.
⁶²*Ibid.*
⁶³*Ibid.*
⁶⁴Fee to Strieby 18 May 1865 AMA 44134.
⁶⁵Fee to Strieby 30 May 1865 AMA 44139.
⁶⁶*Ibid.*
⁶⁷*Ibid.*
⁶⁸*Ibid.*
⁶⁹Fee to Strieby 30 May 1865 AMA 44140.
⁷⁰*Ibid.*
⁷¹Fee to Whiting 9 June 1865 AMA 44144.
⁷²Fee to Whipple 9 June 1865 AMA 44145.
⁷³*Ibid.*
⁷⁴*Ibid.*
⁷⁵*Ibid.*
⁷⁶Scofield to Strieby 15 June 1865 AMA 44148.
⁷⁷*Ibid.;* Collins & Collins, II, 162.
⁷⁸AMA 44148.
⁷⁹Fee to Whipple 27 June 1865 AMA 44149.
⁸⁰John Fee to editor, *Louisville Union,* 7 July 1865, in Howard, *Black Liberation,* p. 128.
⁸¹Fee to Whipple 6 July 1865 AMA 44153.
⁸²Fee to Whipple 19 July 1865 AMA 44160. Brigadier General Clinton B. Fisk was an ardent abolitionist who served on the Executive Board of the AMA

and as Vice-President of the Freedmen's Aid Society of the Methodist Episcopal Church. As assistant commissioner of the Freedmen's Bureau, with jurisdiction over Kentucky and Tennessee, he helped establish Fisk University. His appointment of Fee as superintendent was quite natural, given Fisk's reform sympathies. Henry Lee Swint, *The Northern Teacher in the South* (New York: Octagon Books, Inc., 1967), p. 151.

[83] AMA 44160.
[84] *Ibid.*
[85] Fee to Strieby 2 Aug 1865 AMA 44171.
[86] Clinton Fisk to Fee 4 Aug 1865 AMA 44175.
[87] Williams to Strieby 11 Aug 1865 AMA 44178.
[88] Fee to Strieby 11 Aug 1865 AMA 44179.
[89] Fee to Strieby 16 Aug 1865 AMA 44180; Mary Ann (Thome) Smith Student File [non-gradutate], Box 234, OCA.
[90] AMA 44180.
[91] *Ibid.*
[92] Fee to Strieby 22 Aug 1865 AMA 44184.
[93] *American Missionary*, Vol. IX, no. 10 (Oct 1865), p. 23.
[94] Fee, *Berea*. pp. 49, 50.
[95] *Ibid.*, p. 50.
[96] Wheeler to Whipple 31 Aug 1865 AMA 44187.
[97] *Ibid.*
[98] *Ibid.*
[99] Scofield to Strieby 1 Sept 1865 AMA 44189.
[100] Fee to Whiting 1 Sept 1865 AMA 44190.
[101] Mrs. Colton to Whipple 10 Sept 1865 AMA 44196.
[102] *Ibid.*
[103] Fee to Strieby 15 Sept 1865 AMA 44202-44203.
[104] John Gregg Fee, *Berea: Its History and Work*. published in *Berea Evangelist* 1 Jan 1885-10 June 1886, typescript in Berea College Archives, p. 51; Fee to Whiting 15 Sept 1865 1865 AMA 44204.
[105] Fee to Whiting 15 Sept 1865 AMA 44204.
[106] Fee to Whipple 20 Sept 1865 AMA 44207.
[107] Mrs. Daimon to Strieby 23 Sept 1865 AMA 44209.
[108] Fee to Strieby 26 Sept 1865 AMA 44210.
[109] Fee to Strieby 26 Sept 1865 AMA 44211; Lester Williams to Strieby 27 Sept 1865 AMA 44212; Mrs. Williams to Whipple 28 Sept 1865 AMA 44213.
[110] Fee to Strieby 30 Sept 1865 AMA 44216-44217.
[111] Fee to Strieby 30 Sept 1865 AMA 44216.
[112] Joseph C. Chapin to Whipple 2 Oct 1865 AMA 44221.
[113] Fee to Whipple 2 Oct 1865 AMA 44223.
[114] AMA 44223-44232.
[115] Rev. Edward P. Smith to Strieby 4 Oct 1865 AMA 44229; Mrs. Colton to Whipple 10 Oct 1865 AMA 44234.
[116] Lester Williams to Whipple 18 Oct 1865 AMA 44241; Mrs. Williams' resignation 11 Oct 1865 AMA 44235.
[117] Scofield to Strieby & Jocelyn 20 Oct 1865 AMA 44242; Fee to Strieby 28 Oct 1865 AMA 44244.
[118] Mrs. Daimon to Whipple 20 Oct 1865 AMA 44243.
[119] Wheeler to Strieby 30 Oct 1865 AMA 44248; Fee to Whipple 1 Nov 1865

AMA 44251-44252.

[120]Fee to Whipple 20 Nov 1865 AMA 44260.

[121]*Ibid.*

[122]Large printed map of Berea with pencil notations indicating owners of lots [1887] in Special Collections, Hutchins Library, Berea College; also see James M. McPherson, *The Struggle for Equality: Abolitionists and the Negro in the Civil War and Reconstruction* (Princeton: Princeton U. Press, 1964), pp. 182-3.

[123]Belle Mitchell to Whiting Nov 1865 AMA 44264; Fee to Whipple 2 Dec 1865 AMA 44270. Belle Mitchell continued for a year in her Lexington school. Then in 1867, she taught in a Howard School in Richmond, Kentucky. In 1868, she entered Berea College in the Normal department, where she studied until 1873. She became the second wife of Jordan C. Jackson, a very successful black businessman in Lexington, active in banking, journalism, undertaking and the livery business. He had served as a private in the Civil War (Company E, 5th U.S. Colored Cavalry). From 1879 to 1895 he was a trustee of Berea College, and his son John Henry Jackson, one of Berea's most famous black graduates, also served as a trustee.

[124]Fee to Whipple 2 Dec 1865 AMA 44271; Fee to Whiting 8 Dec 1865 AMA 44277; Rogers to Whipple 2 Dec 1865 AMA 44272; Mary Colton to Whipple 9 Dec 1865 AMA 44278; Wheeler to Whipple 15 Dec 1865 AMA 44281.

[125]AMA 44283.

[126]*Ibid.*

[127]*Ibid.*

[128]Fee to Whiting 6 Jan 1866 AMA 44290.

[129]*Report of the Adjutant General of the State of Kentucky* (Frankfort: John H. Harney, 1867), II, 5. (See Appendix — Camp Nelson: Reverend Abisha Scofield and Reverend Gabriel Burdette.)

[130]Of the 43 surnames borne by men on the Exile Committees of 1859 and 1860, the large-scale slaveowners of Madison County, 31 are also names of black Berea students, 1866-1904. (Actually, hundreds of Berea black students bore those 31 names, some as common as Browning, White, Gentry, Harris, Kavanaugh, Maupin, Miller, Stone: a list which exactly coincides with the standard rollcall of Madison County gentry, the founding settlers from Albemarle County, Virginia.)

[131]Fee, *Autobiography.* p. 178.

[132]Sampson Gentry Civil War Pension File SC479-383 National Archives; Hiram K. Richardson, *Memoirs of Berea* (Berea: Berea College Press, 1940), p. 15.

[133]Scofield to Strieby & Whipple 14 Dec 1866 AMA 44391.

[134]Fee to Whipple 12 Dec 1866 AMA 44387-44388.

[135]*Ibid.*

[136]Fee to Whipple & Cravath 13 Jan 1867 AMA 44407.

[137]*Ibid.*

[138]Fee to Whipple 25 Jan 1867 AMA 44413.

[139]C. C. Vaughn to AMA 16 Feb 1869 AMA 44582; Philip C. Kimball, "Freedom's Harvest: Freedmen's Schools in Kentucky after the Civil War," *Filson Club History Quarterly.* Vol. 54, no. 3 (July 1980), p. 282; 44425; *American Missionary* Vol. XIV, no. 6 (May 1870), p. 127. Later, Berea's black

graduates would have major impact on Kentucky's colored school system, supplying teachers and administrators in great numbers. See, for example, the list of "Colored Graduates," with their occupations, in *Berea Citizen.* 9 Apr 1908.

[140]Fee also sponsored a program for black ownership of land in and around Camp Nelson. He managed with some difficulty to buy 130 acres there and resold it to freedmen in small tracts. Although he tried to induce reformers in Ohio or other Northern states to buy land in Camp Nelson and form a company to parcel out tracts to black buyers, Fee could find no one willing to help. Since his patrimony was spent, his wife sold hers: Matilda Fee divested herself of her inheritance (her father had deeded her land in Indiana), and Fee borrowed an additional $500 to purchase the Camp Nelson land. By 1891, 42 families had established a farm village on this tract. The free church Fee had founded was still there, and Ariel Academy was also operational. *American Missionary.* Vol. 10, 1866 p. 18. Howard, *Black Liberation.* p. 94; Fee, *Autobiography.* pp. 182-183.

[141]*Madison County Deed Book 22.* pp. 85, 145; *Madison County Deed Book 19.* p. 554.

[142]*Map of Madison County. Kentucky* (D. G. Berry & Co., 1876), in the Townsend Room, Crabbe Library, EKU.

[143]This map of Berea, badly worn, but still legible, is in Special Collections, Hutchins Library, Berea College. By 1900 more farms were actually owned by black citizens in Madison County than in any other county in the state. See my *Madison County: 200 Years in Retrospect* (Madison County Historical Society, 1985), pp. 234, 235.

[144]*Madison County Will Book 3.* pp. 171, 436.

[145]John A. R. Rogers, *Birth of Berea College: A Story of Providence* (Philadelphia: Henry T. Coates & Co., 1904), p. 89; Fee, *Berea.* p. 51; Fee, "The Induction of Colored Pupils into Berea College," 2 Aug 1900, MS, BCA.

[146]Ellen Wheeler to Frost Mar 26, 1912 BCA.

[147]Ira V. Brown, "Lyman Abbott and Freedmen's Aid 1865-1869," *The Journal of Southern History.* XV, 34.

[148]Howard, *Black Liberation.* p. 161; Howard, "Negro Politics and the Suffrage Question in Kentucky 1866-1872," *Register.* Vol. 72, no. 2 (Apr 1974), p. 112.

[149]Howard, "Negro Politics," p. 112, *Black Liberation.* pp. 147, 132.

[150]*Black Liberation.* p. 150, 139.

[151]Howard, "Negro Politics," p. 121 & *Black Liberation.* p. 152.

[152]Fee to Whipple 16 Jan 1866 AMA 44295.

[153]Fee, *Autobiography.* p. 12.

[154]Fee to Whipple 6 Mar 1866 AMA 44318; Wheeler to Whipple 22 Nov 1866 AMA 44376; Report of W. W. Wheeler to Berea Board of Trustees 31 Mar 1866 BCA.

[155]Fee to Whipple Jan 1866 AMA 44303; Fee to Whiting 3 Feb 1866 AMA 44305; Richardson, p. 23; Fee to Whiting 11 Apr 1866 AMA 44330.

[156]Fee to Whipple 19 Feb 1866 AMA 44310.

[157]Wheeler to Whipple 22 Nov 1866 AMA 44376.

[158]*Berea Alumnus.* Vol. 4, no. 3 (June 1934), p. 19; *Report of the Adjutant General.* II, 157.

¹⁵⁹Burleigh to Edwin Fee Dec 1924 BCA; Burleigh, *John G. Fee.* p. 10; Angus Burleigh Student File, BCA; Angus Burleigh article, *Berea Citizen.* 25 Sept 1930.
¹⁶⁰Rogers to Whipple (June?) 1866 AMA 44345; UCMB; Burleigh, p. 13.
¹⁶¹Fee to Burleigh 25 Apr 1867 BCA.
¹⁶²Burleigh, pp. 9-11.
¹⁶³Burleigh, p. 11; Burleigh to Edwin Fee Dec 1924 BCA.
¹⁶⁴Burleigh, p. 11; Wheeler to Whipple 22 Nov 1866 AMA 44376.
¹⁶⁵Burleigh to Edwin Fee Dec 1924 BCA.
¹⁶⁶Fee to Whiting 2 May 1866 AMA 44335.
¹⁶⁷AMA 44345.
¹⁶⁸Rogers, p. 94, 96.
¹⁶⁹*Catalogue of the Officers and Students of Berea College 1867-8* (Cincinnati: Elm Street Printing Co., 1868), p. 2.
¹⁷⁰Rogers, p. 97.
¹⁷¹*Ibid.*
¹⁷² Ellen Wheeler to Frost 26 Mar 1912 BCA.
¹⁷³Elizabeth Embree Rogers, "Full Forty Years of Shadow and Sunshine: A Sketch of the Family Life of the J. A. R. Rogers Family," 1896, MS., Berea College Archives, pp. 30, 31.
¹⁷⁴Rogers, p. 99.
¹⁷⁵Elizabeth Rogers, "Full Forty Years," p. 32.
¹⁷⁶*Ibid.*
¹⁷⁷Fee to Whipple 7 Aug 1866 AMA 44349.
¹⁷⁸Fee to Strieby [no date] AMA 44357-44361.
¹⁷⁹Wheeler to Whipple 22 Nov 1866 AMA 44376.
¹⁸⁰*Ibid.*
¹⁸¹*Ibid.*
¹⁸²Fee to Whipple 12 Dec 1866 AMA 44387.
¹⁸³Fee to Strieby 30 Nov 1866 AMA 44378.
¹⁸⁴Fee to Whipple 12 Dec 1866 AMA 44387.
¹⁸⁵Rogers' Report 20 Dec 1866 AMA 44396.
¹⁸⁶*American Missionary.* Vol XII, no. 3 (Mar 1868), pp. 55-57.
¹⁸⁷*American Missionary,* Vol XII, no 61 (Aug 1868), p. 172.
¹⁸⁸*American Missionary,* Vol. XIII, no. 61 (Aug 1869), p. 172. On the basis of Runkle's report, the Freedman's Bureau gave the College $18,000 for the building of Howard Hall. Individual donors were frequently impressed with what they saw or heard of early Berea. Usually they were friends or acquaintances of some Berean — such as J. L. Williston of Northampton, Massachusetts, a friend of Rogers', who gave the school at least $100, then $500 annually, once raising his donation to $1800. Occasionally a donor emerged unknown to anyone — Reverend Lemuel Foster of Illinois was a "surprise" donor who gave a substantial sum when the institution was in great straits. Rogers, pp. 101, 102.
¹⁸⁹*American Missionary.* Vol. XIV, no. 9 (Sept 1870) pp. 207-208.
¹⁹⁰James M. McPherson, *The Abolitionist Legacy* (Princeton: Princeton U. Press, 1975), p. 24.
¹⁹¹McPherson, pp. 245, 246.
¹⁹²Edward Henry Fairchild, *Berea College. Kentucky: An Interesting History* (Cincinnati: Elm Street Printing, 1883), pp. 38, 39.

[193] McPherson, p. 244; Fairchild, *Interesting History.* pp. 63, 64, 66.
[194] Rogers, p. 114; *American Missionary.* Vol. X, no. 11 (Nov. 1865), p. 247.
[195] Fairchild, *Interesting History.* p. 74, 75. p. 115. H. R. Chittenden to Sec. of AMA 22 May 1871 AMA 44802.
[196] E. R., "Full Forty Years," p. 31; Raphael Rogers to Frost 11 Mar 1904 BCA.
[197] Teacher's Reports [Rogers, Berea, Mar 1868], Alvord, *Sixth Report.* quoted in Kimball, "Freedmen's Schools," p. 278; Alvord, "Report," [Jan 1, 1869], pp. 43-49, quoted in Swint, *The Northern Teacher;* Alvord, *Report.* [Jan 1, 1869], pp. 3-4, quoted in Swint, p. 130.
[198] Howard, *Black Liberation.* p. 105.
[199] *American Missionary.* Vol. XV, no. 1 (Jan 1871), p. 2.
[200] Rogers, pp. 128, 130.
[201] Rogers, p. 104; *Historical Sketch of Berea College together with Addresses in Its Behalf by Rev. Jos. P. Thompson. Rev. H. W. Beecher [et al]* (New York: David D. Nicholson, 1869); pamphlet, BCA; Joseph Parrish Thompson, Congregational clergyman, was a founder of the *New Englander* and one of the editors of the *Independent.* See article on him in DAB.
[202] Rogers, pp. 107, 108. Storrs also remarked, "They [the Bereans] have brought both sexes together, young men and young women studying side by side, and this is a thing of great interest and importance." *Historical Sketch.* p. 39. Richard Salter Storrs, Jr., one of the most prominent American clergyman of the nineteenth century, was pastor of the Church of the Pilgrims, Brooklyn, N.Y., for over 50 years. See DAB.
[203] *Ibid.,* p. 107. Dr. Howard Crosby, Presbyterian minister and author, was pastor of the 4th Avenue Presbyterian Church in N.Y.C., and founder of the Society for the Prevention of Crime. See DAB.
[204] AMA 44912.
[205] *Ibid.*
[206] McPherson, p. 245; *Minutes of the Trustees of Berea College.* 2 July 1872, I, 81. John Fee Gregg was the white student whose relationship with a black female student brought the furor about "racial fusion" to a climax. The son of Fee's first cousin, John DeMoss Gregg, John Fee Gregg was brother of the woman who married John T. Robinson, one of Berea's first black graduates. Apparently, Robinson was engaged to one Gregg sister and later married another, after managing the woman's farm in Bracken County for many years. Ernest Dodge, who details this information, is careful *not* to mention the names of either woman, but apparently Robinson married either Laura Ellen or Elizabeth Sarah Gregg. Ernest Dodge to Frost 11 Apr 1925 BCA.
[207] *Chicago Tribune.* 13 June 1874, quoted in Friedman, *Gregarious Saints.* p. 280. Although the Chicago Reunion was primarily a retrospective meeting, a glorification of the abolitionists' past work, Fee characteristically addressed the assembly on the subject of reforming work still to be done. See Larry Gara, "A Glorious Time: the 1874 Abolitionist Reunion in Chicago," *Journal of the Illinois State Historical Society.* LXV (1974), 280-292.
[208] Robinson to Fee Oct 1877 BCA.
[209] *American Missionary.* Vol. III, no. 12 (Dec 1869), pp. 276, 277.
[210] Ernest Dodge to Frost 11 Apr 1925 BCA.

Richard Sears, Professor of English at Berea College, has recently published — in addition to the present study — two books dealing with related subjects: *Madison County: Two Hundred Years in Retrospect,* which places Berea in the context of a county's development, and *The Day of Small Things: Abolitionism in the Midst of Slavery,* dealing with Berea's unique contribution to the abolitionist movement before and during the War Between the States.

Sears holds degrees from the University of Missouri and Ohio University. He lives in Berea with his wife Grace and two sons, Robert and Alden.